XXXIX   WORLD C

The Boston Globe

This book is available in quantity at special discounts for your group or organization. For further information, contact:

Triumph Books
601 S. LaSalle Street
Suite 500
Chicago, Illinois 60605
Phone: (312) 939-3330
Fax: (312) 663-3557

Printed in the United States of America

TRIUMPH
BOOKS
CHICAGO

It's official. Tom Brady follows Joe

Montana into the Pro Football Hall of Fame. The University of Belichick takes its rightful place alongside Harvard and MIT. And the New England Patriots of the 21st century are established as an NFL dynasty on a par with the Packers of the 1960s, the Steelers of the '70s, the 49ers of the '80s, and the Cowboys of the '90s. The Patriots won their second consecutive Super Bowl, and their third in four years, beating the Philadelphia Eagles, 24-21.

PUNTER JOSH MILLER AND COACH BILL BELICHICK TRY ON THEIR NEW HEADGEAR. ADAM VINATIERI GETS A LIFT FROM TEAMMATE CHRISTIAN FAURIA, RIGHT.

CONTENTS

BOOK STAFF

Editor Gregory H. Lee Jr.
Art Director Rena Anderson Sokolow
Designer Tito Bottitta
Photo Editor Jim Wilson
Copy Editor Ron Driscoll
Imaging Frank Briite

Photographers

Jim Davis Pages 3, 7, 8 (bottom), 19, 22, 26, 28, 32, 36, 40 (bottom), 43, 44, 47, 48, 49, 55, 56, 75, 77, 83, 84, 86, 87, 89, 91, 95, 96, 103, 104, 105, back cover.
Matthew J. Lee Pages 8 (top), 9, 11, 20, 34, 50, 51, 52, 53, 63, 64, 71, 72, 76, 78, 79, 80, 81, 92, 99, 100, 101.
Barry Chin Cover, pages 1, 5, 10, 15, 17, 25, 31, 40 (top) 108.
John Bohn Pages 59, 60, 61, 67, 68, 69.
Stan Grossfeld Pages 4, 21, 57, 110.

BY NICK CAFARDO

Triple crown

24-21

NE	0	7	7	10
PHI	0	7	7	7

2/6/2005
59°, CLEAR
ALLTEL STADIUM
JACKSONVILLE

THE RED, WHITE, AND BLUE CONFETTI floated in the sky and dropped ever so gently on their latest field of dreams.

There were hugs, pats on the back, and family moments with children hugging their hero dads, and wives kissing their hero husbands. There were Bill Belichick, Romeo Crennel, and Charlie Weis, the brain trust of the Super Bowl XXXIX champions, embracing for the final time, with Weis off to Notre Dame and Crennel off to Cleveland.

The Vince Lombardi Trophy was touched, kissed, and embraced like a loved one.

The New England Patriots, draped in blood, sweat, and tears, had won the Super Bowl for the third time in four years, beating the Philadelphia Eagles, 24-21, before 78,125 at Alltel Stadium.

Dynasty?

"We're champions now," said Patriots safety Rodney Harrison. "I don't know about dynasty right now."

Football historians will look back upon the current run by the Patriots and decide if it is indeed a dynasty. But for now it's clear that no team in the world is better.

The Patriots broke a 14-14 tie and took control with two fourth-quarter scores against the Eagles, who couldn't stop Tom Brady and Co. when it counted most.

Brady, who played with a heavy heart with his 94-year-old grandmother passing away four days earlier, completed 23 of 33 passes for 236 yards and two touchdowns for a 110.2 quarterback rating. He was the calm, cool quarterback who had been there and done that. His Eagles counterpart, Donovan McNabb (30 of 51 for 357 yards, three touchdowns, and three interceptions), looked jittery at times in his Super Bowl debut.

Brady's favorite target was Deion Branch, who tied a Super Bowl record with 11 catches for 133 yards and was named the game's Most Valuable Player.

"It doesn't make a difference who gets

NEW ENGLAND FIRST DOWNS PHILADELPHIA	RUSHING YARDS	PASSING YARDS	TURNOVERS
21/24	112/45	219/324	1/4

DAVID GIVENS CHECKS HIS FEET TO MAKE SURE HE'S SAFELY IN-BOUNDS ON THE PATRIOTS' FIRST TOUCHDOWN.

SACKS	PENALTIES	TIME OF POSSESSION	RECORD
4/2	7-47/3-35	31:37/28:23	17-2/15-4

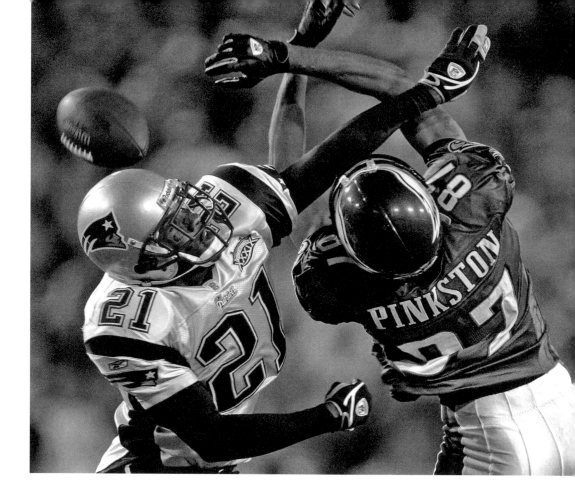

The screen play was successful all game long for the Patriots, none moreso than on the drive that broke a 14-14 tie at the start of the fourth quarter. On first-and-10 at the Eagles' 16, the Patriots lined up three receivers to the left, with only Kevin Faulk in the backfield with Tom Brady. Brady dropped back, looking left the whole time. As the rush closed in, he flared a screen pass on the right to Faulk. Wide open, Faulk ran 14 yards down the right sideline, before being forced out at the 2. Corey Dillon scored on the next play to put the Patriots ahead for good.

what," said Branch. "Our plan was to come in here and win the game. We had a lot of doubters and we showed them that we are a big team and we came out and won tonight."

The Patriots boosted their lead to 24-14 in the fourth quarter courtesy of Adam Vinatieri's 22-yard field goal, which capped an eight-play, 43-yard drive.

McNabb, who has a history of over-throwing receivers at crucial times, got the ball with 5:40 remaining and tried to rally the Eagles.

The Patriots played another stout defensive game, showing McNabb looks — including lining up two linemen and five linebackers — he may have never seen on film. They had to adapt after losing free safety Eugene Wilson for more than half the game with an arm injury.

The Eagles pulled within 24-21 with 1:48 remaining when McNabb found Greg Lewis for a 30-yard touchdown pass over rookie safety Dexter Reid, Wilson's replacement. That capped a 13-play, 79-yard drive that consumed 3 minutes 52 seconds.

The Eagles attempted an onside kick, which was recovered by Christian Fauria at the Eagles' 41. The Eagles forced a Patriots punt, but McNabb couldn't pull off the heroics, with Harrison icing the game with his second interception.

While the Eagles received a strong performance from Terrell Owens (nine catches, 122 yards), the flamboyant receiver never found the end zone.

"Obviously we had a lot of turnovers," said Owens. "My hat goes off to the New England Patriots. They're a good team. It was a hard-fought ballgame. We just gave it away."

"I think we had everyone on the edge of their seats when we went back out there with 50 seconds left. We possibly could have won that game," McNabb said.

But it wasn't to be.

You could sense the Patriots were taking over late in the second quarter, and by the time Paul McCartney had finished "Hey Jude" at halftime, Belichick's troops were ready to carry on the momentum.

Offensive coordinator Weis said the 25-minute halftime allowed him time to figure out how to beat the Philadelphia blitz. He did it with short tosses and screen passes.

The Eagles were still intent on blitzing,

and the Patriots were happy to see it.

"They were blitzing up the middle with [Jeremiah Trotter] in an attempt to make Brady get out of the pocket and so we had to do something to combat it," Weis said.

Brady was picking it up very nicely, spotting Branch for gains of 27 and 21, the latter giving the Patriots a first down at the Eagle 2.

From there, Brady went to designated short-yardage tight end Mike Vrabel, who gathered a tipped pass for his second touchdown reception in as many Super Bowls, giving the champs a 14-7 lead with 11:09 left in the third.

A fired-up Brady returned to the sideline and screamed to his teammates, "Let's keep it going! Let's keep it going!"

Yet the Eagles answered quickly, evening things at 14 with 3:35 remaining in the third. It was turning into a heavy-weight title fight, and McNabb appeared poised for the challenge.

The Eagles targeted rookie corner Randall Gay, throwing at him often during the drive. McNabb completed passes of 15, 4, and 10 yards to Brian Westbrook, the last catch good for 6 points. He also found Lewis and Owens twice each on the drive. His favorite first-half target, Todd Pinkston, was cramping up and was in the locker room receiving intravenous fluids.

The chains kept moving, and even with a blitzing Willie McGinest coming at him, McNabb drilled a pass to Westbrook between two Patriots for the tying score.

With the score even after three quarters (a Super Bowl first), the Patriots started a well-orchestrated drive to regain the lead. Brady was very methodical in leading the Patriots 66 yards, using Kevin Faulk as a key component.

Faulk caught passes of 13 and 14 yards (both beating Eagle blitzes) and ran twice for 20 yards in picking up three first downs on the drive. Corey Dillon capped it with a 2-yard touchdown run off left tackle with 13:44 remaining, giving the Patriots a 21-14 lead.

"We were 0 for 4 on first downs in the first quarter and we really couldn't get into any rhythm offensively," said Brady. "We just didn't move the ball. We tried to run it and didn't gain a whole lot of yards. We made a few more plays in the second half."

At one point in the first quarter, the Eagles led the battle of first downs, 9-1.

The Patriots committed costly penalties early and Pinkston made two beautiful catches on the first scoring drive, which culminated in McNabb hitting L.J. Smith in the end zone with 9:55 remaining in the first quarter.

On their next possession, the Patriots tried to answer, but Brady fumbled when his hand hit Faulk's hip at the Eagles' 5-yard line — New England's first turnover of the postseason.

New England finally scored when Brady hit David Givens for 4-yard score to make it 7-7 with 1:10 left before intermission.

That was not respectable for the three-time Super Bowl champions.

In the end, they adjusted, they executed, and they conquered.

ROOKIE CORNERBACK RANDALL GAY, WHO LED ALL PLAYERS WITH 11 TACKLES, BREAKS UP AN EAGLE PASS, LEFT. RUSS HOCHSTEIN CLEARS A PATH, ABOVE, FOR COREY DILLON'S FOURTH-QUARTER TOUCHDOWN.

THE MVP

BY JOHN POWERS

Record haul

11

RECEPTIONS,
TIES SUPER BOWL RECORD

133

YARDS RECEIVING

12.1

YARDS PER CATCH

HALF AN HOUR AFTER THE PATRIOTS had won their third championship ring, after the fireworks had been set off and the confetti had settled, after he'd been named the Most Valuable Player, Deion Branch still had his gloves on. You never know when Tom Brady might fling another ball his way.

"I don't think they were looking to throw me the ball that many times," said the human Venus flytrap, after he'd caught 11 passes for 133 yards to tie the Super Bowl reception record. But once a wide-open Branch caught one across the middle for 16 yards on New England's first play, he was Brady's favorite target all evening long. "Every time you turned around," said offensive coordinator Charlie Weis, "Deion was catching the ball."

Only San Francisco's Jerry Rice and Cincinnati's Dan Ross had caught that many in a title game, and nobody else has caught 21 in consecutive Super Bowls. "I just try to cash in when I can," Branch said.

Though Brady made a strong case for his third MVP, nobody was arguing that Branch deserved to be the first receiver to win the award since Rice in Super Bowl XXIII and only the fourth overall.

"What can you say?" said Eagles cornerback Lito Sheppard. "The guy stepped up and tied the record."

It was Branch, as much as anyone, who got the Patriots here, burning the Steelers for the first and last touchdowns on a frigid night in Pittsburgh in the AFC Championship Game. And while he didn't cross the goal line here, he kept his teammates chugging along with key catches on every scoring drive. "I was looking to find him today," said Brady. "He was getting open and doing some great things out there."

On the first scoring drive that tied the game at 7-7 late in the second quarter, he caught a 7-yarder for a first down on the Philadelphia 23. On the opening drive of the second half, which Weis and coach Bill Belichick scripted during intermission, Branch caught four passes — for 8, 27, 15 and 21 yards — to set up Mike Vrabel's juggle job for the touchdown that put the Patriots ahead, 14-7.

"He made some nice catches in decent coverage," said Eagles defensive coordinator Jim Johnson. "The ball was right on target. Those were good throws."

But the best of them was the 19-yarder on an in-cut on second and 13 which, combined with a roughing-the-passer call, brought the ball from midfield to the Philadelphia 16. "That was the catch of the game," declared Weis.

That play set up Adam Vinatieri's field goal, which put New England up, 24-14,

with 8:40 to play and provided the victory cushion. "Deion had a great game today," saluted receiver David Givens. "He made some unbelievable catches and ran some great routes. He got open and Tom just put the ball in the right spot."

No man did more to put a third ring on his teammates' fingers, but Branch wasn't claiming sole credit. "It didn't make any difference who won the MVP," he said. "I'm just thankful to be part of this team, man."

Mostly, Branch was thankful just to be in uniform after injuring his knee early in the season and missing two months. "I'm glad that at the time I hurt myself, that Coach Belichick and his staff didn't put me on injured reserve," he said. "They

had the faith that I could come back and contribute to the team. Because if I was on the IR, I wouldn't be standing here."

If his old high school offensive coordinator had his way, Branch never would have put on a helmet. He was too small, too frail. "He kicked me off the middle school team bus because he didn't want me to get hurt," Branch said. "Coach Coleman Kemp. I'm going to put him on the spot. He says to this day he didn't do it. But he did."

No hard feelings from Little Big Man, though. Branch will be glad to give his old coach a ride in his new Caddy, which comes with the MVP. "All the guys will be riding in it anyway," Branch figured. ◥

▰ DEION BRANCH TOES THE LINE IN THE SECOND QUARTER AFTER ONE OF HIS RECORD-TYING 11 RECEPTIONS.

MIKE VRABEL
MR. VERSATILE

BY BOB HOHLER

Quite a catch

2

YARD TOUCHDOWN CATCH,
WHICH BROKE A 7-7 TIE
IN THE THIRD QUARTER

2

TACKLES,
ONE FOR A LOSS

1

SACK,
FOR A 16-YARD LOSS

TRUTH BE TOLD, TOM BRADY WOULD rather toss a Super Bowl touchdown pass to almost anyone but Mike Vrabel. At least that's the way Vrabel described their relationship after the Patriots linebacker cameoed as a receiver and snagged a touchdown pass from Brady in a second straight Super Bowl.

"Tom gets mad at me in practice and won't throw it to me," Vrabel said after his acrobatic catch helped the Patriots win their third Super Bowl in four years. "But during the game, he didn't have a choice."

In the natural order of football, quarterbacks have little love for linebackers, even their own.

"I'm always yapping at him in practice as part of 'The Dirty Show,'" Vrabel said, referring to New England's scout team. "So he doesn't like it when I come over on offense."

Good thing Brady follows his game plan rather than his emotions. With the Patriots slogging through a 7-7 deadlock early in the third quarter, Vrabel improved his career receiving record to a perfect 5 for 5 (all touchdowns) when he broke free of Philadelphia strongman Jevon Kearse's clutch in the end zone and hauled in Brady's 2-yard throw. Vrabel also lined up as a tight end last year and snared a fourth-quarter touchdown pass

from Brady to help the Patriots defeat the Carolina Panthers in the Super Bowl.

"What started out as a gimmick certainly has somewhat evolved into an every-game, every-week package," Vrabel said, holding his 3-year-old son, Carter, on his knee after the game. "I'm just fortunate to be part of it."

While the strategy has become common for the Patriots in goal-line situations, Vrabel's catch was the most spectacular of his limited but high-profile career as a receiver. Kearse wrapped up Vrabel so tightly he was called for a holding penalty, yet Vrabel managed to break free and make the diving catch.

"Jevon was hanging all over me and pulling me down from the back," Vrabel said. "I was lucky enough just to tip it up and hang onto it when I hit the ground."

In a playful impersonation of a Terrell Owens touchdown dance, Vrabel celebrated by flapping his arms as if he were one of Philadelphia's "dirty birds." But the arm-flapping routine may also have been aimed at some of his team's detractors.

"We stood up to a lot of challenges and put up with the stigma of being these average guys who went out there as pieces for Bill Belichick," Vrabel said. "We have great coaches, but we also have great players that go out and play hard."

DESPITE BEING HELD ON THE PLAY, MIKE VRABEL BROKE LOOSE TO CATCH A TD PASS IN A SECOND STRAIGHT SUPER BOWL.

RODNEY HARRISON

THE LEADER

BY KEVIN PAUL DUPONT

Survivors

2

INTERCEPTIONS,
INCLUDING ONE IN THE CLOSING
SECONDS TO SEAL THE GAME

7

TACKLES,
SECOND-HIGHEST ON THE TEAM

1

SACK,
FOR A 1-YARD LOSS

LIFE IN THE NEW ENGLAND SECOND-ary isn't necessarily a ticket out of town, but a career as a Patriot pass snatcher is a sure path to perdition.

Welcome to the troubled job market, Eugene Wilson.

The talented safety became the latest casualty when he exited with an arm injury in the second quarter of Super Bowl XXXIX. Wilson was hurt while trying to trip up speedy kickoff returner J.R. Reed.

Having played without key secondary components Ty Law and Tyrone Poole for a long stretch this season, the already-compromised secondary had to shift down yet another gear.

Next to tiptoe up to the abyss: rookie Dexter Reid.

"I told him, 'Hey, we need you. You have to step up,'" Rodney Harrison, the leader of the challenged bunch, said he told Reid at halftime. "That's it. I told him, 'You have to go out there and play, and if you don't get the job done on one play, it doesn't matter. Get up for the next one and move on.'"

One more time, the patchwork Patriots secondary was equal to the task. There was indeed a dropoff without Wilson, and that was evident with 1:48 to go in the fourth quarter when wide receiver Greg Lewis eluded Reid and snared a 30-yard Donovan McNabb TD pass.

Fittingly, though, it was the work of the secondary that ultimately put the finishing touch on the third Super Bowl title in four years. McNabb, working from the Philadelphia 5-yard line, took the snap with 17 seconds to go, and fired a pass that was tipped into Harrison's arms near the 28. He advanced the ball 6 yards, hit the ground, and promptly broke into a celebratory, arms-waving dance around the field.

"That was a tough-fought game," said Harrison, whose final moments in last year's victory were far more subdued after he exited with a broken arm. "I'll tell you, I was nervous back there, with Donovan in control of the ball with 17 seconds to go. He's capable of making a play with his legs as well as his arm. There's still the chance that maybe he hits T.O. [Terrell Owens] on a 70-yard slant and he takes it to the house."

In part, said Harrison, it was breaking that tension that led to the dance. "I was just so happy the game was over," he said. "Before that throw, I was telling our guys, 'Stay deep ... stay deep and deeper.'"

Harrison, for one, was expecting more of a T.O. show. "To do what he did today, that was incredible," said Harrison, referring to Owens's gallant return, which was against the advice of the orthopedic sur-

geon who repaired his ankle Dec. 22.

For extra incentive this time around, the veteran Harrison had Eagles wide receiver Freddie Mitchell. The former, and oft-disappointing first-round draft pick irked Harrison during a recent ESPN interview when he said he couldn't name the members of New England's secondary. He said he only knew Harrison, and he would have something waiting for Harrison at the Super Bowl. Not surprisingly, Mitchell never seemed to cross Harrison's path.

"Of course it did," said Harrison, asked if Mitchell provided him with extra incentive. "I told our guys, 'Go out there now and make people know your number. Show the world who you are — this is a wonderful stage to do it.' I bet you he knows who they are now."

ASANTE SAMUEL AND RODNEY HARRISON CAN FINALLY RELAX — AND LET OUT A WHOOP — AFTER HARRISON'S INTERCEPTION WITH 9 SECONDS LEFT IN THE GAME.

17

THE DYNASTY

BY BOB RYAN

Without doubt, they're the best

COULD THERE POSSIBLY BE ANY MORE doubts?

The best team in football has just concluded a grueling four-week exam period in which it faced three completely different challenges from three very good football teams. You can make a case — in fact, I'm going to — that this was the most difficult postseason task ever presented to a team attempting to win a Super Bowl.

The grades? A-plus, A-plus, and A-minus. The scores? 20-3, 41-27, and, finally, 24-21. Yup, for the third time in four years the Patriots have become the champions of the known football universe with a 3-point victory. But 3 or 30, it doesn't matter. The idea is to score more points than the other guys, and no team this century has found the weekly formula to do just that better than the New England Patriots.

Think about it: The New England Patriots are the unquestioned Team of the Century.

They are now in the enviable position of being able to judge championships. The first was, obviously, sweet. The second was vindicating and harrowing. But this one demanded a level of overall excellence that should make everyone involved feel incredibly proud. For what the Patriots have done in defeating these three particular teams in four weeks is nothing short of awe-inspiring.

"Indianapolis, we all know what kind of a team they are," said Bill Belichick. "Pittsburgh was the best team in the AFC all year. Philadelphia went wire-to-wire all year. I can't think of three tougher teams in my experience in the postseason."

This was a Patriots season unlike any other. After getting off to a 6-0 start, the entire season was threatened by the devastation of the secondary, forcing Belichick and his defensive staff to start improvising with players and schemes that made them the talk of both the NFL and the world of football in general. The brain trust had to make do with a converted wide receiver, a converted linebacker, and assorted people from the waiver wire. They kept winning and they made it look easy.

It was not.

The secondary nightmare continued right through last night, when starting free safety Eugene Wilson injured his

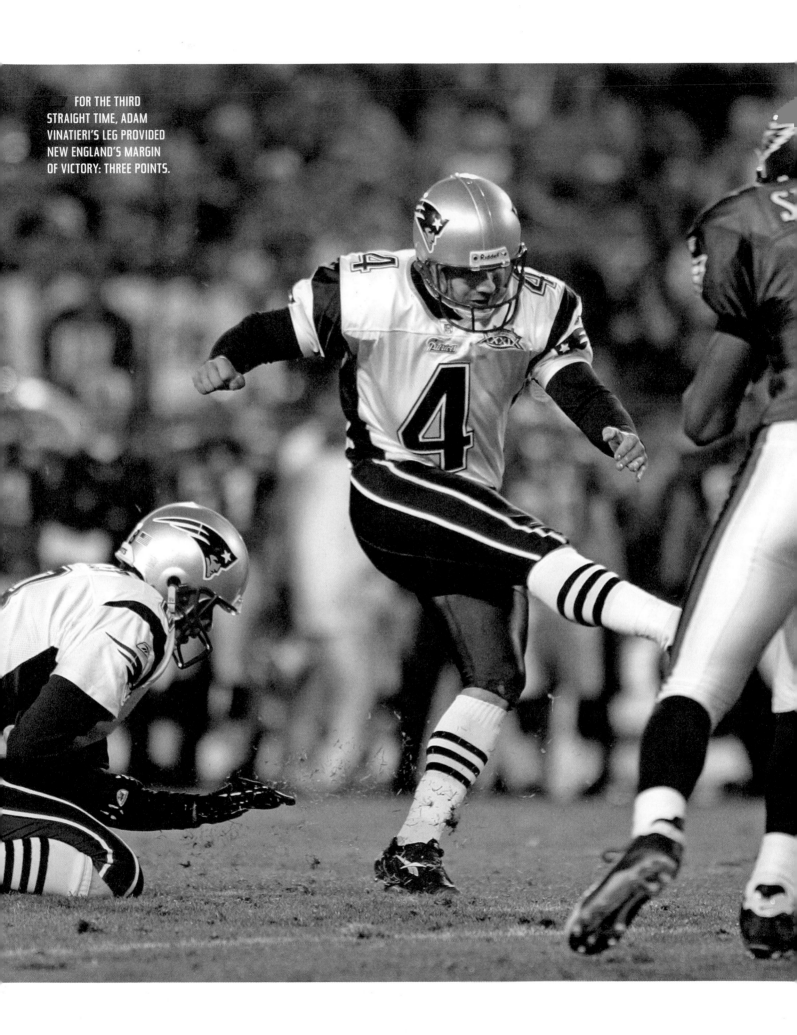

FOR THE THIRD STRAIGHT TIME, ADAM VINATIERI'S LEG PROVIDED NEW ENGLAND'S MARGIN OF VICTORY: THREE POINTS.

arm while performing special teams duty late in the second quarter. This vaulted rookie Dexter Reid, a fourth-round pick from North Carolina, into the lineup. Were there scary moments? Oh, yes. Greg Lewis beat him for a touchdown in the fourth period, but the only thing that mattered was that he wasn't beaten more. He was good enough to get the job done, and on this team, Getting The Job Done is the only criterion for maintaining employment.

But it wasn't easy, and finding a way to compete with the personnel at hand may have been the toughest challenge of Belichick's coaching career.

"I can't say enough about these players," said Belichick. "These guys have worked so hard for the last six months. They just stepped up, kept working, kept fighting, and they did it again today."

This game was work. The Eagles came completely as advertised defensively, holding Tom Brady & Co. to one first down and no points in the first quarter. Brady looked curiously uncomfortable in the kind of Big Game that has made his reputation.

It didn't last, of course, because Tom Brady really is Mr. Cool, and it was only a matter of time before he and his mentor, Charlie Weis, found out what would and wouldn't work against an aggressive, speedy Philly defensive unit. With the typical Patriot lack of flamboyance, the offense calmly executed five excellent drives after falling behind, 7-0.

The first ended in frustration when Brady botched a handoff to Kevin Faulk and wound up fumbling the ball away after he had apparently recovered it. But three of the next four possessions resulted in marches of 37, 69, and 66 yards for touchdowns and the following drive culminated in a 22-yard field goal by Adam Vinatieri that provided the Patriots with the eventual margin of victory.

We are used to seeing Brady do whatever is necessary to win. He is now 9-0 in three playoff visits. But Philadelphia defensive coordinator Jim Johnson apparently needs to see just a little more before he becomes a true Brady admirer. "Brady is on his way to being one of the better quarterbacks," he noted.

Thanks, coach. We'll keep our eye on him.

All week long, people peppered Belichick with questions about whether a third Super Bowl championship in four years would constitute a dynasty, and all week long he responded to such queries with the verbal equivalent of a stiff-arm. Naturally, people wanted to know if he would care to comment on that possibility now.

"We don't look at it that way," he explained. "We didn't look at it that way two days ago and we don't look at it that way now. We started out like everyone else — at the bottom of the mountain, and now we're at the top. When next season starts we'll start out at the bottom again."

Well, coach, how do these championships differ?

"If it's a scale of one to 10," he said, "they're all tens."

This season has to go down as an 11. The Patriots went 14-2 in the regular season, with the Pittsburgh loss loaded with asterisks and the second Miami game a complete giveaway. And leave it to Belichick to point out that "we also beat both of those teams, so we can say we took [on] and defeated all comers."

They also peaked at precisely the right time, playing brilliant all-around games against the Colts and Steelers and then probing and adjusting against the Eagles until getting the thing calibrated just so.

We can get started with the historical judgments in due time. Right now all that needs to be said is that the Patriots once again met every challenge and are — how great does this sound? — the Team of the Century.

Make sure to leave early enough for a good spot at the parade. ◄

DONOVAN MCNABB IS FORCED TO THROW AROUND AN ONRUSHING TEDY BRUSCHI IN THE SECOND QUARTER.

KING OF THE WORLD
DAVID GIVENS HAS REASON TO STRUT AFTER
CATCHING TOM BRADY'S SECOND-QUARTER PASS
FOR NEW ENGLAND'S FIRST TOUCHDOWN.

STEELERS

BY NICK CAFARDO

Bus stopped

41-27

NE	10	14	7	10
PIT	3	0	14	10

1/26/2005
11°, FAIR
HEINZ FIELD
PITTSBURGH

SEVEN MINUTES AND SEVEN SECONDS remained in the first quarter when it became evident that the Patriots were going to win the AFC title at Heinz Field.

The Steelers had decided to go for it on fourth and 1 at the Patriots' 39-yard line. It wasn't the biggest or the most important play because it came so early, but it seemed to crystalize what the Patriots, who were about to win their third AFC Championship in four years, were all about.

Before the Steelers came up to the line of scrimmage, coach Bill Belichick summoned middle linebacker Ted Johnson and offered some advice. Johnson, who calls the defensive signals, took that advice back to the huddle. Moments later, Jerome Bettis took a handoff from Ben Roethlisberger and was stopped dead in his tracks by Roosevelt Colvin, who stripped the ball loose. Mike Vrabel made the recovery.

"[Belichick] saw something and he alerted me and it turned out to be huge. It was an adjustment — I really can't go into it," said Johnson. "That stuff happens all the time. It's amazing sometimes."

So many small things added up to a 41-27 win over the Steelers, sending New England to Super Bowl XXXIX in Jacksonville. If the Patriots have a to-do list, you can be sure every item has been checked off.

New England stopped the Steelers' inside running game, holding Bettis to 64 yards on 17 carries. They rattled Roethlisberger, who had three interceptions, including one that was returned 87 yards for a touchdown by Rodney Harrison, boosting the visitors' lead to 24-3 late in the first half. The Pats solved Pittsburgh's vaunted zone blitz as Tom Brady, who improved to 8-0 in the postseason, had another of his money games, completing 14 of 21 attempts for 207 yards, a pair of touchdowns, no interceptions, and a 130.5 passer rating.

In addition to Harrison and Brady, Deion Branch and Corey Dillon also came up with big plays. Branch caught four passes

	FIRST DOWNS		RUSHING YARDS	PASSING YARDS	TURNOVERS
NEW ENGLAND	18/19	PITTSBURGH	126/163	196/225	0/4

THE PATRIOTS WRAP UP JEROME BETTIS, WHO RAN FOR JUST 64 YARDS ON 17 CARRIES IN THE AFC CHAMPIONSHIP GAME.

SACKS	PENALTIES	TIME OF POSSESSION	RECORD
1/2	1-5/2-20	28:29/31:31	16-2/16-2

DEION BRANCH IS FAR AND AWAY AS HE HAULS IN A TOM BRADY PASS FOR A 60-YARD SCORE IN THE FIRST QUARTER. IT WAS THE LONGEST PASSING TOUCHDOWN IN NEW ENGLAND POSTSEASON HISTORY.

for 116 yards and a touchdown and rushed twice for 37 yards and another score. Dillon rushed 24 times for 73 yards, including a huge 25-yard scoring run in the third. Let's not forget a pair of interceptions by Eugene Wilson and a Heinz Field record-tying 48-yard field goal by Adam Vinatieri.

It was as if the Patriots sent a gift to millions of New Englanders trapped in their homes as a result of the weekend blizzard.

"This is for all the fans," said Patriots owner Bob Kraft, who accepted the Lamar

Hunt Trophy after the game from AFC representative Joe Namath. "We have the greatest fans in the country and we know that the weather is tough up there and we wanted this for them."

The Patriots created their own blizzard on the field. They had been smacked around in a 34-20 loss here on Halloween. All week they had watched film of how badly they had played. The Patriots were embarrassed and you can be sure Belichick reminded them plenty.

"We played Patriots football," nose tackle Keith Traylor said. "We were physical from the opening play. We came out with an attitude and they fought back. Coach [Bill] Cowher's teams never quit and they didn't."

The Patriots' 21-game winning streak ended here Oct. 31, but last night the Patriots ended Pittsburgh's 15-game win streak in what was a far more devastating loss.

Traylor was right about the Steelers not quitting. Pittsburgh scored two touchdowns and a field goal to pull within 11 points with 13:29 remaining.

Both teams were aided by overturned plays on challenges which led to scores.

The Steelers got their break when David Givens made what appeared to be a 44-yard catch over the middle for a first down at the Steelers' 28. But before Brady could run the next play, Cowher tossed the red beanbag and officials overturned the call, ruling the ball hit the ground. That forced the Patriots to punt.

The Steelers started at their 45 following a 22-yard return by Antwaan Randle El and drove to the New England 2. But on fourth and goal, Cowher sent in Jeff Reed, who drilled a 20-yard field goal.

"I think with 13½ minutes to go, to only be down by 11 points, which is just two scores — a field goal, a touchdown, and a 2-point conversion — I thought there was too much time to go with 2 yards to come away with nothing. That was my decision and I would do it again," Cowher said.

The Patriots had received a big break on another play involving Givens, who had caught an 18-yard pass and appeared to fumble. Officials ruled cornerback Willie Williams had recovered, but a look by the replay judge revealed that Givens's knee had hit the ground. A 15-yard unnecessary roughness penalty on Clark Haggans was tacked on.

On the next play, Dillon, who had been contained quite nicely by the Steelers, ran around the right side behind Stephen Neal for a 25-yard touchdown to give the Pats a 31-10 lead.

The Steelers had scored on their first possession of the third quarter when Roethlisberger, whose right hand had been soothed with cold water late in the first half, came out with an air of confidence. He led the Steelers on a five-play, 56-yard drive, the big play a 34-yard pass to Randle El. Bettis took it in from the 5.

Harrison's 87-yard interception return for a touchdown, which made it 24-3 with 2:14 remaining in the first half, broke the Steelers' back. Roethlisberger stepped back and tried to throw it to the right side to tight end Jerame Tuman. Harrison jumped the route, snagged the pass, and was helped by a Mike Vrabel block on Roethlisberger as he jogged, then walked, into the end zone.

"That was at least a 10-point swing, maybe more," Belichick said.

The Patriots had gone ahead, 17-3, on a five-play drive in which Brady connected on a 46-yard pass and great catch by Branch, who caught the ball while getting hit by Troy Polamalu at the Steelers' 14.

Two plays later, Brady appeared to check off at the line when he spotted the defense playing off Givens. Brady hit Givens with a quick toss, freezing Williams, who slipped and allowed Givens to run 9 yards untouched into the end zone.

The Patriots forced two early turnovers, the first when Wilson picked off Roethlisberger's first pass. The rookie overthrew Randle El for his eighth interception in his last 87 throws.

The first of two Branch reverses — the second one resulted in a 23-yard touchdown run in the fourth — seemed to loosen the Steeler defense. That led to Vinatieri's long field goal.

It was after the big fourth-and-1 stop of Bettis in the first quarter that Patriots offensive coordinator Charlie Weis went for the jugular.

Starting at his 40, Brady hit Branch in stride at about the 5-yard line and the speedy receiver stumbled in from there. Brady made the play work when he looked over the middle, which drew Polamalu over and left Branch alone with Deshea Townsend. The 60-yard touchdown reception is the longest in Patriots postseason history. ⌁

OVERJOYED
PATRIOTS OFFENSIVE LINEMAN MATT LIGHT
SIGNALS THE FINAL NEW ENGLAND TOUCHDOWN
WHILE PITTSBURGH'S KIMO VON OELHOFFEN
CAN'T BEAR TO LOOK.

DIVISIONAL PLAYOFF
COLTS

BY NICK CAFARDO

Stopped Colt

20-3

IND	0	3	0	0
NE	0	6	7	7

1/16/2005
25°, CLOUDY, SNOW
GILLETTE STADIUM
FOXBOROUGH

ALL WEEK THE MESSAGE WAS CLEAR. "You have to slow him down," said the experts. "You have to get him out of his rhythm." The Patriots went one better — they stopped Peyton Manning cold.

Maybe the signs and the chants were a little harsh during New England's 20-3 pounding of the Colts and Manning, which punched New England's ticket to the AFC Championship Game in Pittsburgh.

"After the game you will get your ring — suffer-ring," read one. The crowd was yelling "Cut that meat! Cut that meat!" in reference to Manning's ad campaign in which he cheers for the common folk while they're performing their jobs.

The NFL MVP was just that yesterday — common. Manning, (27 of 42, 238 yards, one interception) was unable to lead his vaunted offense to the end zone, and his longest completion was 18 yards.

The Patriots, who were without Pro Bowl defenders Ty Law and Richard Seymour, played it the way some experts thought they would — jamming receivers at the line, rushing three, occasionally sending a blitzing linebacker to knock Manning off his rhythm, and covering well. They never allowed the Colt receivers to get free downfield. They disguised their defense by sometimes dropping eight men into coverage and sometimes going with as few as four defensive backs.

The Colts coaching staff had no answers. It also had no answers for the steady snow that fell throughout the game, accompanied by a swirling wind.

The Patriots also adopted another much talked-about suggestion — they controlled the clock for 37:43 with three massive scoring drives of 16, 15, and 14 plays which ate up a total of 24:47. Two of the lengthy drives came in the second half when the Patriots completely took over.

Corey Dillon carried 23 times for 144 yards, while Tom Brady played a mistake-free game, completing 18 of 27 passes for

NEW ENGLAND	FIRST DOWNS	INDIANAPOLIS	RUSHING YARDS	PASSING YARDS	TURNOVERS
	21/18		210/46	115/230	0/3

IT'S DEJA VU ALL OVER AGAIN. NFL MVP PEYTON MANNING CAN SEE THAT HE IS ABOUT TO FALL TO 0-7 AGAINST THE BILL BELICHICK-COACHED PATRIOTS, AND 0-2 IN PLAYOFF GAMES.

SACKS	PENALTIES	TIME OF POSSESSION	RECORD
1/3	5-35/4-44	37:43/22:17	15-2/13-4

13:42
4TH QUARTER

The Patriots had used a time-consuming drive to take a 13-3 lead into the fourth quarter but the game was still in the balance. Facing a third-and-10 from their 6-yard line with 13:46 to play, Tom Brady lined up in the shotgun with only Kevin Faulk in the backfield. Faulk came out of the backfield and juggled the ball, but made an 11-yard catch for the first down that kept alive a drive that would lead to the game's final touchdown and an insurmountable 20-3 lead.

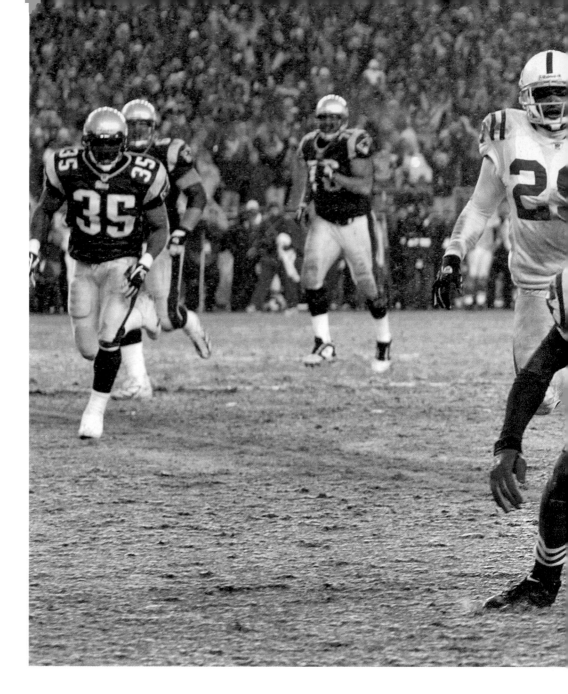

144 yards, one score, and no interceptions.

The Patriots seemed buoyed by Mike Vanderjagt's "ripe for the picking" comment earlier in the week. They were buoyed by the media members who dismissed their chances of stopping the Colts.

"I guess the panel of experts were wrong, huh?" said Matt Light, who shrugged off an early illegal motion penalty on a fourth and goal at the 1-yard line, which nullified a Corey Dillon touchdown and ultimately cost the Patriots 4 points after they settled for Adam Vinatieri's 24-yard field goal.

The Patriots converted 53 percent (8 for 15) on third down, including 6 of 8 in the second half. As has been their trademark, they made big plays at big times.

None was bigger than Tedy Bruschi's strip of Dominic Rhodes at the Patriots 39-yard line with 3:18 remaining in the second quarter. Bruschi wrestled the ball away after Rhodes caught a Manning pass for a 2-yard loss.

The Patriots easily could have gone into the half trailing, 7-6, but the defense forced the Colts to settle for Vanderjagt's 23-yard field goal as time expired. It was the one time Manning had been able to sustain a long drive. Manning connected on passes of 13, 16, 11, and 10 yards during the 11-play, 67-yard drive, which nearly ended on an interception, but the ball slipped through Eugene Wilson's hands in the end zone.

"We would have liked to have gotten a

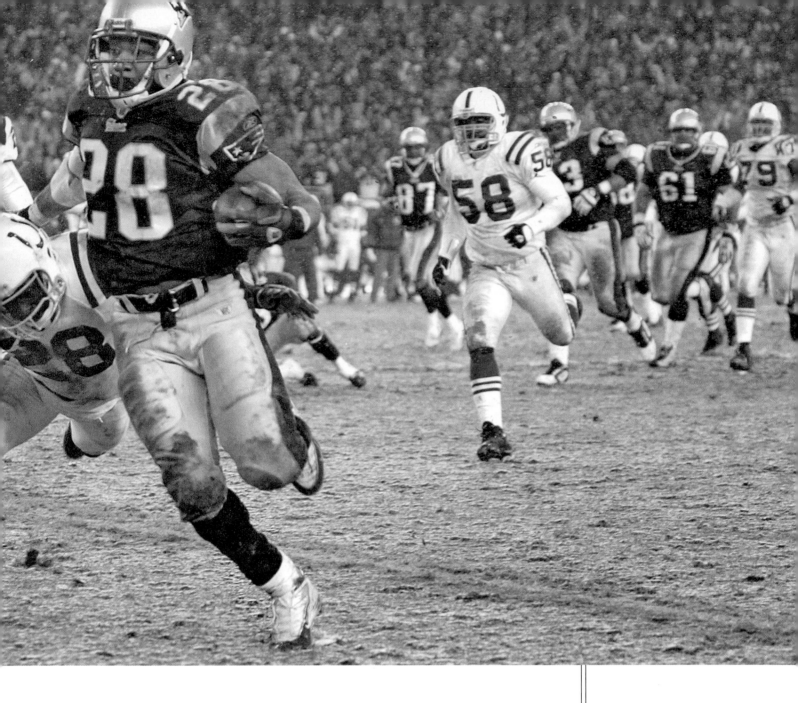

touchdown there," Colts coach Tony Dungy said. Holding the Colts to a field goal over the first 30 minutes was amazing enough. The Patriots did it with Asante Samuel blanketing Marvin Harrison, Randall Gay shadowing Reggie Wayne, and Brown covering Brandon Stokley.

The linebackers took turns on tight end Dallas Clark. Elder statesman Roman Phifer, not known for his coverage skills, did an admirable job.

"We heard all week we couldn't cover all of their guys, but I think we did a good job," said Samuel, who did a solid job filling in for Law, holding Harrison to five catches and 44 yards. Both teams had futile series to open the second half, but the Patriots settled in and played what Bill Belichick called "our best 30 minutes of football." Beginning a drive at their 13, the Patriots steadily used Dillon and Kevin Faulk to move down the field. They got a big 14-yard pass play from Brady to Patrick Pass on a third-and-3, which advanced it to the Indianapolis 24. And then it was Faulk and Dillon to the 5, where Brady hit David Givens for the first touchdown of the game. The drive took 8:16 off the clock.

"Everyone doubted us," said Patriots defensive end Jarvis Green, who filled in so admirably for Seymour. "They said we couldn't do it. It was very emotional for us. The last two years have been great. We won 28 games and lost only four." ◄

COREY DILLON RUMBLES TO THE COLTS' 1-YARD LINE, SETTING UP TOM BRADY'S TD PLUNGE THAT CAPPED A 7-MINUTE, 24-SECOND GAME-CLINCHING DRIVE.

KNOCKOUT PUNCH
TOM BRADY EXULTS AFTER CONNECTING WITH DAVID GIVENS FOR A 5-YARD TOUCHDOWN THAT CAPPED A 15-PLAY DRIVE WHICH ATE UP MORE THAN HALF OF THE THIRD QUARTER AND GAVE THE PATS A 13-3 LEAD.

COLTS
CARDINALS
BILLS
DOLPHINS
SEAHAWKS
JETS
STEELERS
RAMS
BILLS
CHIEFS
RAVENS
BROWNS
BENGALS
DOLPHINS
JETS
49ERS

BY JOHN POWERS

Their image

RUSHING OFFENSE	PASSING OFFENSE	SCORING OFFENSE	TURNOVER RATIO
133.4/7th	224.2/11th	27.3/4th	+9/8th

is everything

ART ROONEY II STEELERS PRESIDENT

SOCRATES, WHO LIVED BACK AROUND the time of Papa Bear Halas, had the championship formula figured out a couple of millennia before Super Bowl I. "Know thyself," the Greek philosopher preached.

Pro football teams and their followers may talk about philosophies, systems and programs, but success and failure essentially are questions of self-knowledge. In the NFL, identity usually determines destiny.

"Knowing who you are and what you want to be," muses ABC Sports analyst John Madden. "What is an Oakland Raider? What is a Seattle Seahawk? What is a Dallas Cowboy? If you can't answer that, therein lies the problem. What is an Arizona Cardinal? I have no idea."

By now, after winning two Super Bowls in three seasons, the Patriots have an identity that is recognized far beyond Foxborough. "Intelligent, efficient, businesslike, physical, adaptable, flexible," says Giants general manager Ernie Accorsi. "Play well in the clutch, win tough road games..."

The storied professional football franchises, such as Green Bay, Pittsburgh, Miami, Dallas, San Francisco, never had a problem with mistaken identity. The Packers were about discipline and professionalism, the 49ers about flair and imagination, the Cowboys about innovation and precision, the Dolphins about poise and resourcefulness, the Steelers about smashmouth straightforwardness.

Even the new franchises, whose trophy cases still are bare, have identities-in-progress. "Our identity is, we play hard," says Houston Texans general manager Charley Casserly. "If you come to play us, it's a 60-

INTELLIGENT, EFFICIENT, BUSINESSLIKE, PHYSICAL, ADAPTABLE, FLEXIBLE...

ERNIE ACCORSI GIANTS GM

RUSHING DEFENSE	PASSING DEFENSE	SCORING DEFENSE	PENALTIES
98.2/6th	212.5/17th	16.2/2nd(t)	101/6th

minute football game."

The Patriots are about focus, pragmatism, diligence, versatility, resilience, selflessness. "They aren't a team of superstars," says Pittsburgh president Art Rooney II, whose team handed the Patriots the first of their two defeats this season and has now twice lost to them for the right to go to the Super Bowl. "They're not looking for the other guy to make the play."

For most of their 45 years, the Patriots had a negative identity. They were the Patsies, fortune's fools, playing beneath a persistent rain cloud. Silly things happened to them, most of their own making. "They were No. 4 in that town forever," says Casserly of Boston's four major pro teams. He spent a decade in Springfield as a student, coach, and administrator. "And it wasn't close between 4 and 3."

The slapstick image began changing in 1993 when Bill Parcells was hired, and the Patriots went from 2-14 to the Super Bowl in four seasons. "They hired a proven winner who had won two Super Bowls," says Casserly, who was with the Redskins when they won three titles. "That gave them a new identity immediately."

THERE IS A PATRIOT WAY NOW...
BILL WALSH FORMER 49ERS COACH

The Patsies persona vanished three years ago when New England upset the St. Louis Rams for its first championship. The new persona, built around preparation and passion, was reinforced last February when the Patriots defeated the Carolina Panthers for their second crown.

"The way Bill Belichick is doing it right now is the best way," says Kansas City Chiefs coach Dick Vermeil, who made it to the Super Bowl with both the Eagles and Rams. "They're winning the most football games, so that makes it the best way."

With their AFC title victory over Pittsburgh, the Patriots have won 31 of their last 33 games. That stretch included a league-record 21 straight wins, which Belichick saw as 21 one-game winning streaks. His team's record, he says, is now 0-0, just as it was last year at this time. That approach — an obsession with what's dead ahead — is what makes the Patriots who they are now. What-ifs don't concern them.

"It's a core part of our philosophy," says Patriots vice president Scott Pioli, who's in charge of player personnel. "Hypotheticals don't matter. It's wasted time, wasted energy, rather than what's real and what's right in front of you."

The Belichick credo is practical, absolute: "Whatever it is, it is." If Drew Bledsoe goes down, if the linebackers and cornerbacks start dropping, you plug in different people and you deal with it.

"You just try to take the situation at hand and do the best you can with it," says Belichick. "When it is over, recalibrate, reload, and go again. That is where we have been all season. We never sat there and thought, 'Well, if this happens, where are we going to be two months from now?' We just never look at it like that."

The schedule says you play on Sunday and the rules say you must have 11 men on the field. Sometimes, that means using a receiver as a cornerback. But you show up and you perform, however you must.

"You just think about, 'Here's who we're playing this week. What are we going to do? What is our best chance to do it?' " says Belichick. "You jump off the ship and you start swimming. You don't really worry about where you are going. You are just trying to make good time."

It's not as if the Patriots plunge overboard without a life preserver, a compass, and shark repellent. What sets them apart from most of their rivals is that they're meticulously prepared and that everyone — from owner Bob Kraft to Belichick to the assistant coaches to the scouts to the players to the trainers to the equipment people — is on the same page.

"They have the strongest philosophy in those terms," says Madden, who coached the eye-patched Raiders (has any team had a clearer identity?) to their first Super Bowl victory. "This is the way you play football as a New England Patriot. This is how you play on offense. This is how you play on defense. This is how you play on special teams. They have a system for everything and they teach it better than anybody."

There is a Patriot Way now, just as there has been a Packer Way, a Dolphin Way, a Cowboy Way, a 49er Way, a Steeler Way. All

THE WAY BILL BELICHICK IS DOING IT RIGHT NOW IS THE BEST WAY. THEY'RE WINNING THE MOST FOOTBALL GAMES, SO THAT MAKES IT THE BEST WAY.

DICK VERMEIL CHIEFS COACH

of them revolve around what former San Francisco coach Bill Walsh calls "a central belief system."

Some, like Pittsburgh's, which is based on robust running and uncivil defense, go back decades. "Even when we didn't have very good teams, people would say that even if the Steelers didn't beat you, you felt like you'd gotten beat up after you played them," says Rooney.

Much of the Steeler identity comes from having had one owner (the Rooney family) for their 71 years and only two coaches (Chuck Noll and Bill Cowher) since 1969. When Kraft bought the Patriots in 1994, they had had three owners, four coaches, and four quarterbacks in seven years. "Stability and continuity are critical," says Pioli.

Now they've had the same owner for 11 years, the same head coach for five, the same quarterback for four. But equally significant is the stability and continuity of expectations. There's no confusion, no dissension, about how to reach their goals. "We do what we say we're going to do," says Pioli.

The clarity and simplicity of purpose comes from Belichick, who has been around long enough now to shape his team in his image.

"For better or worse, it's impossible for a football team not to take on the personality of its head coach," says Accorsi. "You can see that the Steelers are Cowher and that the Patriots are Bill."

Pro football isn't primarily about philosophies and systems, about schemes and tendencies, playbooks and scouting reports.

"It all starts with people," says Vermeil. "You have to have a foundation of things you believe in. You have concepts and philosophies that you operate by. But I always start with people. Then, I worry about how we're going to do things."

The challenge, for the Patriots and everybody else in the league, is finding what teams call "our kind of guy."

"Everyone wants big, fast, tough, smart guys who love the game," says Jacksonville executive scout Terry McDonough, who worked with Belichick and Pioli in Cleveland.

The Patriots clearly know what they don't want. "A player who has limited ability and a player who is a bad character guy," says defensive coordinator Romeo Crennel. "If you fit that criteria, you don't fit in."

What the Patriots are looking for are players with football character.

"We're concerned about what the players are like as people and what things are important to them," says Pioli. "What their overall makeup is, what motivates them, how much pride they have. Essentially, how important football is to them. There's no test that will tell you that. It's a combination of observing, of asking questions, of gathering information."

The core question is: Can he be a Patriot? Will he buy into what we're doing? Can he fit in here?

"We're not for everyone, and not everyone is for us," says Pioli.

The three Patriotic essentials are commitment, focus, and discipline.

"Being where you're supposed to be when

BILL AND SCOTT START WITH BRINGING IN OUR TYPE OF GUYS. THEN OUR JOB IS TO FIT THEM IN... WE NEVER LOOK AT A PLAYER AS SOMEBODY WE CAN'T USE.

CHARLIE WEIS PATRIOTS OFFENSIVE COORDINATOR

ROMEO CRENNEL PATRIOTS DEFENSIVE COORDINATOR

you're supposed to be there and doing your job," says Pioli. "That's what discipline is."

By that standard, Tom Brady is the team's star-spangled poster boy. Even during the bye week, he was thinking "all day, every day" about all three of New England's potential playoff opponents.

"What is the price you would pay for success?" he muses. "What would you give up to win this game?"

Brady was the 199th player chosen in the 2000 draft. Who would have predicted that he would quarterback the team to two Super Bowls?

"I don't think we would have been talking about Brady like that before the 2001 season," says Belichick. "Who is this guy? Some guy from Michigan? A sixth-round pick? What's the big deal about him?"

The big deal was Brady's intangibles (a word the Patriot brass dismiss; every quality is tangible, they insist). No quarterback in the league manages a game better. But that wasn't obvious until Drew Bledsoe got hurt and Brady stepped in.

"It's a very unscientific business at times," concedes Belichick. "That's why there are so many mistakes in the draft, in personnel

The Belichick philosophy is that football players play football. Why can't Mike Vrabel catch touchdown passes? Why can't kicker Adam Vinatieri throw them? Why can't tight end Christian Fauria defend on Hail Mary plays? Why can't receiver Troy Brown fill in at cornerback?

"If you use a purist approach, you get in all kinds of trouble," says Walsh, who coached the 49ers to three Super Bowl victories and is now a special assistant to the athletic director at Stanford. "I always took the position that if a player has a redeeming quality, then he can help us."

If a player is athletic, intelligent, and adaptable, the Patriots see no reason why he can't play a different position, can't step up when needed.

"Everyone on that team has a role," says Madden. "Everyone is treated like a starter and everyone is taught to be a starter. In practice, they'll put in a backup linebacker and a backup safety to work with their No. 1 defense. So when there's an injury and the backup goes in, he's been there before."

The Patriots' remarkable ability to be whatever they have to be on a given Sunday has made them difficult to label. They aren't

FOR BETTER OR FOR WORSE, IT'S IMPOSSIBLE FOR A FOOTBALL TEAM NOT TO TAKE ON THE PERSONALITY OF ITS HEAD COACH.
ERNIE ACCORSI GIANTS GM

and free agency. Put guys in different systems, put them in different opportunities, it turns out differently."

You don't have to be a top draft pick to start for the Patriots. Wide receiver David Givens was a seventh-round pick, center Dan Koppen a fifth. But the Patriots had a sense they would blossom in Foxborough.

"Bill and Scott start with bringing in our type of guys," says offensive coordinator Charlie Weis. "Then our job as coaches is to fit them in. Don't say, 'Well, he can't do this.' Find out what he can do. We never look at a player as somebody we can't use."

"The Greatest Show on Turf," they have no "Steel Curtain" or "Doomsday Defense." They just know how to put one W after another. That's the Patriot Way.

Parcells, who has logged 16 seasons as a head coach with four NFL teams, has a theory about football identities. "You are what you are," he likes to say.

If you're 2-14, you're 2-14. And if you're 14-2 . . .

The Patsies who used to live at this address were somebody else. These Patriots have rings on two fingers and are going for a third. They are what they are. ◀

41

BY NICK CAFARDO

Wide right

27-24

IND	0	17	0	7
NE	3	10	14	0

9/9/2004
73°, CLOUDY
GILLETTE STADIUM
FOXBOROUGH

IN THE END, YOU COULD ARGUE THAT the only team that could stop the Indianapolis Colts was the Indianapolis Colts, but then you wouldn't be giving due credit to two incredible defensive plays by Eugene Wilson and Willie McGinest.

As hard as Edgerrin James ran in the season opener, he coughed up the football twice when the Colts had chances to score, none more critical than at the Patriots' 1-yard line late in the fourth quarter. As James put his head down and ran straight ahead, Wilson poked the ball out, and rookie Vince Wilfork recovered to preserve the Patriots' 27-24 win.

It extended the Patriots' win streak to 16 games, two short of the NFL record, and it certainly wasn't easy. The Patriots trailed, 17-13, at halftime in a game that featured superb offensive performances by Tom Brady (26 of 38, 335 yards, three touchdowns), David Patten, and Corey Dillon.

Trailing, 27-17, after three quarters, the Colts began their comeback, taking advantage of Ty Law's injury as Tyrone Poole and Asante Samuel were the corner-backs covering the Colts' dangerous receivers. Poole and Mike Vrabel were flagged for interfering with receivers, and Law, who implored coach Bill Belichick to let him back in the game, finally was allowed to return, only to give up a 7-yard touchdown pass from Peyton Manning to Brandon Stokley to make it 27-24 with 11:05 remaining.

The Patriots made two consecutive mistakes — a Brady interception by Nick Harper and a Deion Branch muff of a punt, which gave the Colts great field position and set up James's goal-line fumble. The Colts then foiled the Patriots' attempt to run out the clock, and when Manning found Stokley for a 45-yard completion, the Colts were deep in New England territory. After a crushing 12-yard sack by McGinest, Mike Vanderjagt missed a 48-yard field goal wide right with 24 seconds remaining.

Predictably, offensive coordinator Charlie Weis had the Patriots come out passing the ball against a young and depleted Colts secondary. Brady completed passes of 19 yards (to David Givens), 14 (to Branch), and 14 (to Ben Watson) as the Patriots quickly found themselves at the Colts' 10-yard line, before a delay of game penalty forced them to settle for Adam Vinatieri's 32-yard field goal.

The Colts responded with an impressive drive of their own, starting at their 28 and moving to the Patriots' 6. The big

NEW ENGLAND	FIRST DOWNS	INDIANAPOLIS	RUSHING YARDS	PASSING YARDS	TURNOVERS
	22/28		82/202	320/244	2/3

DAVID GIVENS WAS ON THE RECEIVING END OF TOM BRADY'S FIRST COMPLETION OF THE SEASON.

SACKS	PENALTIES	TIME OF POSSESSION	RECORD
1/2	8-55/3-20	28:19/31:41	1-0/0-1

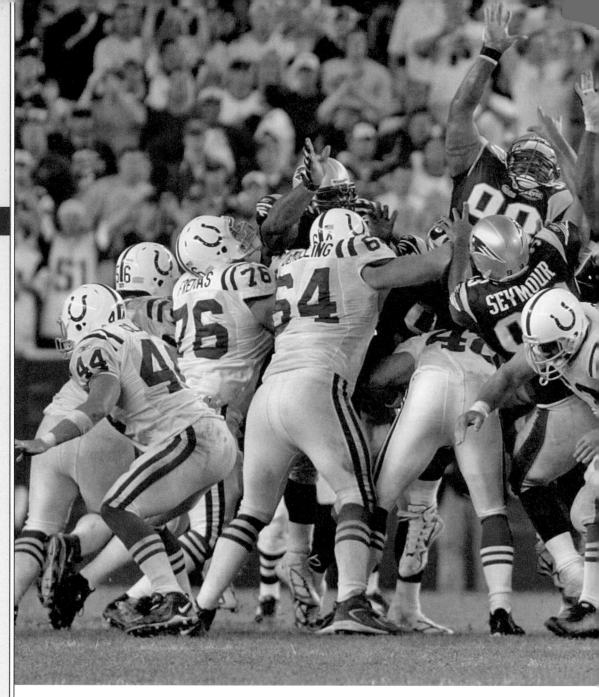

:24

4TH QUARTER

Facing third and 8 at the Patriots' 17, the Colts had a chance to win or tie. But Peyton Manning was sacked for a 12-yard loss by Willie McGinest, turning a chip-shot field goal for Mike Vanderjagt into a 48-yard attempt. He missed wide right, and New England escaped with a 27-24 victory.

play was a 42-yard hookup from Manning to Reggie Wayne, who was lined up in the slot against Vrabel and easily beat the linebacker down the field. The Colts were running effectively with James between the tackles, but just when you thought they would stick with what was working, Manning dropped back to pass.

Ty Warren got strong pressure up the middle and forced Manning to throw into a crowd of Patriot jerseys near the goal line. Tedy Bruschi came up with the interception, foiling the Colts' chance to tie or take the lead.

On the Colts' next series, Manning con-nected with James for 6 yards, Marvin Harrison for 9, and James for 20 to the Patriots' 29. The Colts advanced as far as the 14, but Manning's third-down pass to Harrison in the end zone was broken up by Wilson. Vanderjagt came on to make his 42d consecutive field goal, from 32 yards with 13:44 remaining in the second quarter.

Upon getting the ball back, the Colts ran it on nine consecutive plays, with James and Dominic Rhodes busting through the Patriots' defense at will. Rhodes capped the drive from 3 yards with 8:02 remaining in the half, giving

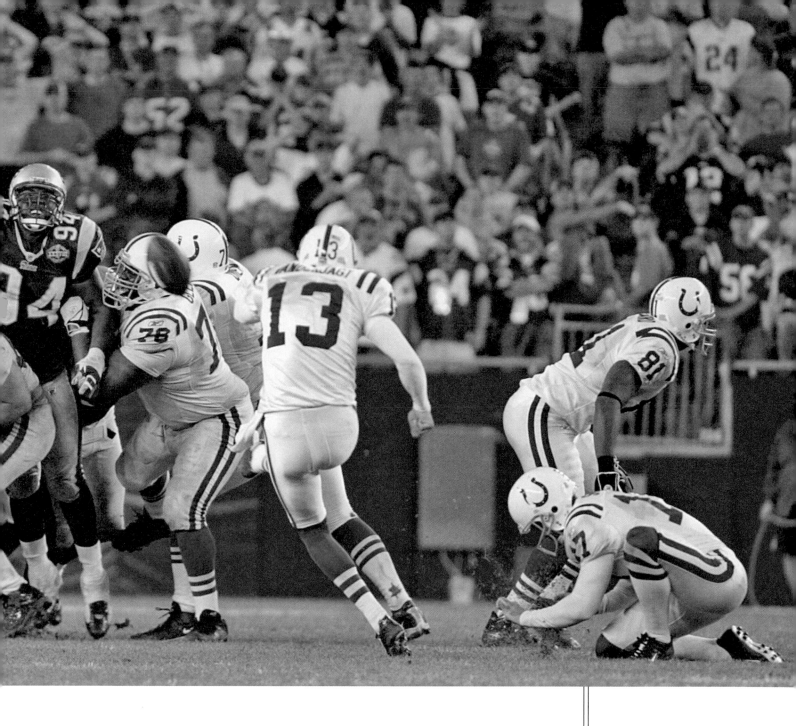

the Colts a 10-3 lead, the first time the Patriots had trailed in a regular-season game since falling behind, 20-13, to the Houston Texans Nov. 23, 2003.

Not to be outdone, the Patriots showed off their new toy — Dillon. Adrian Klemm threw a nice block that sprung Dillon for a 38-yard gain. Once Dillon blasted through the front seven, he made a move, leaving Idrees Bashir in the dust. Brady found Branch for the tying score with 4:04 left before intermission.

But the Colts kept having their way with the Patriots' defense. They eventually regained the lead on Manning's 3-yard pass to Harrison just over the goal line on the right side of the end zone.

A nifty 34-yard kickoff return by Bethel Johnson set up Vinatieri's 43-yard field goal as time expired, bringing the Patriots within 17-13 at the half. They came out with a sense of urgency in the second half, the defense stopping the Colts on three plays on the first series. The offense also appeared more determined. Brady struck for gains of 12 and 17 yards to Branch, and Dillon bounced off a tackler for a 10-yard gain before Brady spotted Patten open in the end zone and hit him in stride as the Patriots took the lead, 20-17.

COLTS
CARDINALS
BILLS
DOLPHINS
SEAHAWKS
JETS
STEELERS
RAMS
BILLS
CHIEFS
RAVENS
BROWNS
BENGALS
DOLPHINS
JETS
49ERS

23-12

NE	7	7	3	6
AZ	0	6	6	0

9/19/2004
89°, CLOUDY
SUN DEVIL STADIUM
TEMPE

BY NICK CAFARDO

Not pretty

ONE OF THESE DAYS A RISING TEAM like the Arizona Cardinals is going to come out of the blue and beat the defending Super Bowl champions, but this wasn't going to be the day.

The Cardinals might have been pesky and tough, the 100-degree heat on the field posed some problems, and the emotional halftime tribute to Pat Tillman gave the Patriots all they could handle, but New England has made winning a habit and an art form.

The Patriots probably should have given the Cardinals a thumping, but still extended their winning streak to 17 with a 23-12 triumph over the Cardinals before a crowd of 51,557.

The Patriots had the majority of the crowd behind them in what was a quasi home game, and they certainly had all the sexy statistics in their favor, including Corey Dillon's 158 yards on 32 carries, and David Givens's 118 receiving yards on six catches. The Cardinals' Josh McCown was sacked five times in the first half while being held to a 33.7 quarterback rating, and

the Patriots defense held the Cardinals to 167 total yards, only 50 net yards rushing.

The defense was out there for 11 Cardinals possessions. Four of them were three-and-out, two of them netted negative yardage, and only two drives were more than 40 yards in length as New England held Arizona to one touchdown.

"I have to say congratulations to Bill Belichick and his team," said Cardinals coach Dennis Green. "Winning 17 games in a row is absolutely incredible. It was a very physical football game."

The win, which was followed by a week off, wasn't good enough for some of the Patriots, especially not quarterback Tom Brady, who threw two touchdown passes to Daniel Graham but also threw two interceptions.

"We left a lot of plays out there and we have stuff we're going to have to correct," Brady said. "I think the way we're playing is not going to be good enough much longer."

The day wasn't that easy for the 2-0 Patriots, but it was never that hard, either.

"We just wanted to be aggressive, come after them hard, make their quarterback make some tough reads, and stop the run," said Patriots defensive lineman Richard Seymour, who was a stalwart on the three-man line along with Vince Wilfork and Ty Warren, who were rotated with Keith Traylor and Jarvis Green later on.

The Cardinals (0-2) mounted their best drive of the game for almost eight min-

	FIRST DOWNS	RUSHING YARDS	PASSING YARDS	TURNOVERS
NEW ENGLAND / ARIZONA	24/14	172/50	205/117	3/2

ASANTE SAMUEL AND EUGENE WILSON BOTH GET A RISE OUT OF WILSON'S SECOND INTERCEPTION OF THE GAME.

SACKS	PENALTIES	TIME OF POSSESSION	RECORD
5/2	12-79/6-43	35:16/24:44	2-0/0-2

COREY DILLON BREAKS THROUGH THE CARDINAL LINE ON THE WAY TO A SEASON-HIGH 158 YARDS RUSHING. AT RIGHT, WILLIE MCGINEST POUNCES ON ARIZONA'S JOSH MCCOWN FOR ONE OF FIVE NEW ENGLAND SACKS.

utes of the third quarter, going 80 yards after Adam Vinatieri had hit a 29-yard field goal, one of his three on the day.

After Ty Law was called for pass interference on Bryant Johnson in the end zone, placing the ball at the 1, Emmitt Smith powered in to cut the gap to 5 points, 17-12. The Cardinals went for 2, and couldn't take advantage of the Patriots having only 10 men on the field as McCown had a receiver open in the end zone and never saw him.

As it turned out, the Law penalty didn't haunt the Patriots as the defense tightened up and forced the Cardinals into consecutive three-and-outs in the fourth quarter.

Good fortune certainly played a part in the win.

On their first scoring drive, Patrick Pass caught a little swing pass from Brady and gained 30 yards before a bunch of Cardi-

nals forced the ball loose. As the ball trickled down the field, toward the left sideline, two Cardinals and one Patriot converged. It appeared to be an Arizona recovery.

But somehow Deion Branch squeezed in between the two and came up with the ball just inside the 10. Brady capped the drive with a 2-yard touchdown pass to a wide-open Graham.

That successful series seemed to illustrate the fact that the Patriots were superior in all aspects. The Cardinals weren't struggling for lack of trying; they were simply undermanned. The Patriots' defense began to rise up, pressing McCown into a bad interception when he tried to force it to rookie Larry Fitzgerald.

Eugene Wilson picked it off at the 44 and returned it to the Arizona 30.

Before you could check the temperature,

Brady found a wide-open Graham for a 19-yard touchdown pass on third and 19 just 1:44 into the second quarter.

"It's just like we drew it up in practice," Graham said. "Nothing different. We practiced that play all week in practice, and we went out and executed it."

The defense was on display in the second quarter after Dillon fumbled a pitch from Brady and Arizona recovered and ran it to the Patriots 11. They had first and 10 at the 11 and wound up with a fourth and 32, and needed a 51-yard field goal from Neil Rackers just to salvage 3 points.

The usually mistake-free Brady threw an ill-advised ball as he was being hit by nose tackle Russell Davis, forcing an underthrow to Givens. Cornerback David Macklin picked it off and returned it to the Patriots 42.

The defense was stingy, and Rackers hit a 52-yard field goal, making it a 14-6 game as the temperature, which was 89 at game time, reached 100 degrees on the field.

A game that certainly appeared would be a blowout after the Patriots went out to a 14-0 lead, wasn't. The Cardinals were young, tough, and fast, as advertised. They just didn't have enough experience or manpower to match the Patriots, who are in a habit of winning.

A habit that's hard to break. ⬥

PLAY OF THE

GAME

13:16

2ND QUARTER

The Patriots scored their second touchdown (and the eventual winning points) after a penalty left them in a third-and-goal situation at the Cardinals' 19 early in the second quarter. The Patriots did it by giving the Cardinals too much to do on the right side of the field. TE Daniel Graham slipped through on the same side to make a 19-yard touchdown haul.

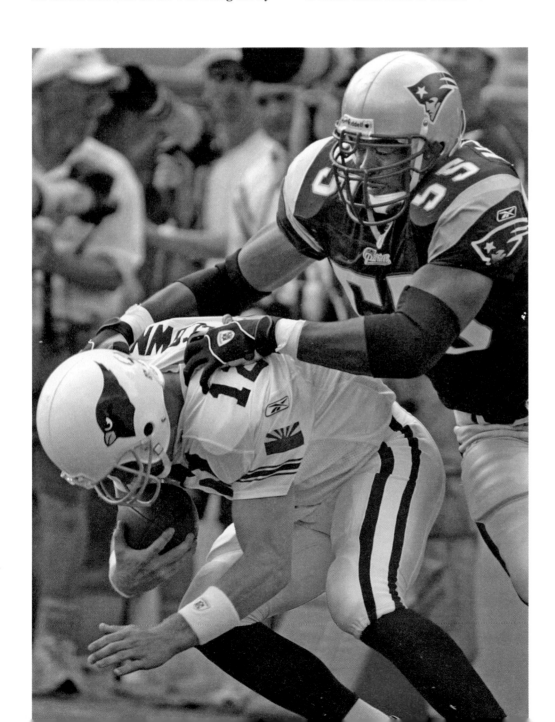

BY NICK CAFARDO

18-Wheeler

31-17

NE	10	7	0	14
BUF	10	7	0	0

10/3/2004
58°, SUNNY
RALPH WILSON STADIUM
BUFFALO

◥ MIKE VRABEL SALUTES DANIEL GRAHAM'S GO-AHEAD TD CATCH IN THE FOURTH QUARTER.

TOM BRADY WALKED OUT OF THE Patriots locker room to the podium in the interview room at Ralph Wilson Stadium smiling, and why not? Though he's not supposed to think about it, the team he quarterbacks had just won its 18th straight game, a 31-17 triumph over the Bills, tying the record for the most consecutive wins including postseason games.

In some locker rooms that would have been cause for champagne streaming through the air, a celebration of a remarkable record that, with one more victory, would be all theirs. Miami also won 18 straight including postseason, in 1972 and '73, including an undefeated '72 season.

But in New England's locker room, the only thing the players were doing while getting dressed was trying to dodge the media and questions about the streak.

"Better standing up here now than last year [after a 31-0 loss]," Brady joked. "We had a lot of penalties and missed opportunities, but we settled in in the second half. They have a very good team."

Once again, when it really counted, in

a game that was tied at 17 and anyone's to win for three-plus quarters, the Patriots seized the moment. In the end they played like Super Bowl champions; the Bills played like a team in disarray and likely heading for some major changes, perhaps even the unseating of Drew Bledsoe at quarterback.

The Patriots were confident if it came down to the end, they could rattle Bledsoe. While they spared him most of the game, they blitzed him into oblivion in the fourth quarter. If they were banking on Bledsoe's teammates not being able to bail him out, they were right.

"We just wanted the ball to come out fast," said Patriots strong safety Rodney Harrison, who was relentless at the end. "Our front guys really did a wonderful job putting pressure on Drew. We didn't play very well in the first half, but in the second half we made some adjustments and we

FIRST DOWNS
NEW ENGLAND 21/18 BUFFALO

RUSHING YARDS
99/138

PASSING YARDS
298/199

TURNOVERS
1/2

RICHARD SEYMOUR PICKS UP THE BALL AND RUNS WITH IT, ALL THE WAY TO A CLINCHING 68-YARD FUMBLE RETURN. IT WAS HIS FIRST NFL SCORE.

SACKS	PENALTIES	TIME OF POSSESSION	RECORD
7/0	10-77/11-94	28:43/31:17	3-0/0-3

were able to pull out a very tough divisional win in a very tough place to play."

The game was iced with New England ahead, 24-17, late in the fourth quarter. The Bills drove to the Patriots' 17 where Bledsoe took a fourth-and-3 snap, faked a handoff to Travis Henry, and never saw Tedy Bruschi bearing down on him, unabated. Bruschi knocked the ball loose and Richard Seymour picked it up and lumbered 68 yards for the clinching score.

"I'm just glad I got into the end zone," Seymour said. "I'm not used to running that far, but you always like scoring touchdowns when you're a defensive player."

The Bills were running a bootleg for Bledsoe, believing it was a play the Patriots would least expect.

They were probably right, except it looked like Bledsoe was merely dropping back and starting to roll right before Henry allowed Bruschi to come clean and Bruschi knocked the ball loose.

Buffalo wide receiver Eric Moulds had a different take on the play.

"It was a situation where I think Travis went the wrong way," said Moulds. "Drew was supposed to hand it off to him, but Travis went the wrong way, and Drew never really got a chance to put the ball

away. The guy hit him, made the play, and [they] scored."

Henry, who ran well for 98 yards on 24 carries, had back-to-back regrettable plays. He tripped on a third and 2 from the Patriot 16 before he could hit what looked to be a hole and get the first down, then missed the blocking assignment.

Of the fourth-down play, Henry said, "I think it was a run play, and I was faking the run, so I don't know what happened, or why [Bruschi] came up the middle like that, but it was miscommunication somewhere."

Bledsoe was more direct. "If we had executed the play correctly, hopefully Bruschi would have tackled Travis on the play fake and it would have been there," he said.

With an 0-3 start in his first NFL head coaching job, the Bills' Mike Mularkey lost his composure when a reporter asked whether it was a good idea to run Bledsoe on a rollout.

"I think it is," Mularkey said. "Knowing what I know compared to what you know."

Earlier in the final quarter, the Patriots went on an 80-yard scoring drive, helped by another Bills brain burp.

Buffalo had stopped the drive and forced Adam Vinatieri to kick a 31-yard field goal, but on the attempt Rashad Baker was offside, allowing the Patriots to continue the drive. Brady later found Daniel Graham on a 2-yard touchdown pass, with Graham making a nice snatch low to the ground.

Could the outcome have been reversed if a couple of plays had gone differently? Absolutely.

Ask London Fletcher what he was thinking when he picked up a loose ball in the fourth quarter after New England's David Givens seemed to catch a pass but then had the ball stripped.

Fletcher ran it down the right sideline, but was caught by the Patriots' Bethel Johnson and tried to lunge into the end zone.

At that point, the Patriots' Stephen Neal blasted Fletcher, and the ball went flying through the end zone for a touchback, which would have been Patriots' ball. The Bills threw a replay flag and got the officials eventually to reverse the Givens fumble to an incomplete pass.

However, if Fletcher had just gone down at the 2, the Bills might have been able to tie it because the Patriots were out of challenges.

Fletcher left the locker room without speaking to the media.

The Patriots had a bad day on special teams, allowing a 98-yard kickoff return by Terrence McGee with 1:26 remaining in the first quarter, tying the game at 10. They also allowed a 34-yard run on a muffed snap by punter Brian Moorman, who grabbed the loose ball and ran to the Patriot 41, from where Bledsoe made his best play of the game — a scoring strike to Moulds that gave the Bills a 17-10 lead with 2:43 remaining in the half. The Patriots then tied it on a 30-yard pass from Brady to David Patten with 1:28 left before intermission.

On the ensuing kickoff, the Patriots had decided they didn't want to kick to McGee, and Vinatieri tried to hit the ball to the side, but it hooked out of bounds. The ball came out to the Buffalo 40, but Bledsoe and the Bills went three and out.

Brady was pleased to take a knee and get to the locker room with a tie, a far cry from how the game started. New England began the contest by marching 77 yards on nine plays, capped by Corey Dillon's 15-yard run right up the middle.

Dillon, who ended with 79 yards on 19 carries, also fumbled at the Bills 2-yard line in the second quarter on a big hit by Chris Kelsay.

Which is why the Patriots were content to take their chances in the second half, where they have pulled it out so many times in their 18-game streak. 🏈

DAVID GIVENS SLIPS BEHIND SAFETY COY WIRE FOR A 44-YARD GAIN TO SET UP NEW ENGLAND'S FIRST TOUCHDOWN IN THE FIRST QUARTER.

BY NICK CAFARDO

Broken record

24-10

MIA	0	7	3	0
NE	7	10	7	0

10/10/2004
64°, CLOUDY
**GILLETTE
STADIUM**
FOXBOROUGH

THERE WAS NO CHAMPAGNE-SPRAYING celebration in the Patriots locker room following their historic 24-10 victory over the Miami Dolphins. In fact, the only person who got wet was coach Bill Belichick, who received a Gatorade shower from Richard Seymour and Rodney Harrison in the final seconds.

A smiling Belichick acknowledged the crowd with waves to every side of the stadium, shook hands with most of his players for their part in the 19-game winning streak, including postseason, gave out some attaboys, and then, according to Harrison, the coach said, "However, we have a great Seattle team coming in."

End of celebration.

The Dolphins really didn't defend the honor of the 1972 team, the only one to go undefeated in a season and one of the teams that had won 18 straight. In fact, Miami (0-5) is closer to becoming a winless team than it is to resembling its '72 forebears.

This wasn't one of the 19 straight that will be remembered as an artistic success,

NEW ENGLAND	FIRST DOWNS	MIAMI	RUSHING YARDS	PASSING YARDS	TURNOVERS
	14/18		135/67	69/228	1/2

BEWARE THE STRAIGHT ARM: COREY DILLON CHUGS 36 YARDS TO SET UP A THIRD-QUARTER TOUCHDOWN. HE WAS THE GAME'S LEADING RUSHER WITH 94 YARDS.

SACKS	PENALTIES	TIME OF POSSESSION	RECORD
3/1	7-55/12-86	28:58/31:02	4-0/0-5

10:37
3RD QUARTER

Corey Dillon was the Patriots' main offensive weapon against Miami and set up New England's final touchdown (a 1-yard Rabih Abdullah plunge) with a bruising 36-yard run on a third-and-2 early in the third quarter. The Dolphins defense lined up with five men in the box plus blitzing linebacker Junior Seau, while the Patriots had Dillon alone in the backfield. New England tackle Matt Light picked off the charging Seau and Dillon ran through the vacated hole. Miami linebacker Zach Thomas read the play perfectly and met Dillon just beyond the line of scrimmage. Dillon, however, bounced off the hard-hitting Thomas and continued to rumble down the sideline.

and the Patriots haven't had one of those in their first four games. But they do enough to get the job done, and yesterday was no exception.

Down three receivers because of injuries to Troy Brown (shoulder) and Deion Branch (knee), and the benching of Bethel Johnson, and dealing with injuries, including the one to cornerback Tyrone Poole, the Patriots were playing reserves at key positions. At times one could see Dexter Reid at safety, Randall Gay (who had an interception) at corner, Kevin Kasper at receiver and kick returner, or Rabih Abdullah at tailback.

The Dolphins had their own problems, losing kicker Olindo Mare (right calf) before the opening kickoff, forcing punt returner Wes Welker to handle kickoff, extra point, and field goal duties. Welker, who had minimal kicking experience at Texas Tech, booted a 29-yard field goal and nailed an extra point. And late in the fourth quarter, the Dolphins lost two quarterbacks in three plays.

Starter Jay Fiedler suffered a rib injury on a 12-yard sack by Harrison. Two plays later, A.J. Feeley took a shot to his ribs on an incomplete pass to Chris Chambers on fourth and 7 and probably would not have come back had the Patriots not been able to run out the clock.

The New England defense made three exceptional red-zone stands in the fourth quarter.

"We just didn't want to give up those points," Harrison said. "It was just a matter of pride. Guys came up with plays, and

time and time again that's the character of this team."

Cornerback Ty Law said he got himself motivated by all the hype about the Miami defense throughout the week. Law said he didn't want to leave the game without feeling the Patriots' defense had outplayed Miami's.

"I'm playing against another corner [Sam Madison] over there, and I want to come out of it having the better game," said Law.

That wasn't hard for Tom Brady to do, as his counterpart, Fiedler, missed throw after throw.

Brady didn't hit many either, completing 7 of 19 for 76 yards, marking the first time since Oct. 7, 2001 he had thrown for fewer than 100 yards. But two of the completions went for touchdowns.

The Dolphins tried to take a page from the Bills' game plan and blitz Brady repeatedly. They got some good licks on him, especially one by Jason Taylor that bloodied Brady's chin, but only defensive tackle Dario Romero sacked him.

The game seemed to turn on one play by Miami punter Matt Turk. The Dolphins cut the Patriots' lead to 10-7 when Fiedler threw a 10-yard touchdown pass to Chambers, but on Miami's next possession Turk took a snap slightly to his left and panicked.

Instead of trying to punt, he elected to tuck the ball and run for a first down. On fourth and 7, he fell 4 yards short.

The Patriots took over at the Miami 46 and marched for a score on Brady's 5-yard toss to David Givens to make it 17-7 at the half.

"I have no idea," said Dolphins coach Dave Wannstedt when asked why Turk ran. "He said the snap was a bit high, which it was, but you need to kick the ball. He's got to make the decision looking at the whole picture. I don't think anyone was rushing him. He just instinctively took the ball and ran."

Turk said he had problems handling the ball, "and I thought it was too late to try and kick it, when actually I probably could have. It was a bad play."

After the game, Wannstedt struggled to explain what has happened to this once-proud franchise.

"We continue to not give ourselves a chance to win," he said. "We don't make

enough on offense and we are just making too many negative plays. We make a first down and somebody jumps offside. We were giving them a short field to operate. It's frustrating for everyone."

The Patriots scored in the first quarter thanks to a nifty interception by Gay with which he ran 10 yards to the Miami 30. Brady found Givens for a 12-yard reception on third and 8 to the Miami 16. A roughing-the-passer call on a blitzing Will Poole helped the Patriots get a first down at the Miami 14. Corey Dillon ran for 12 yards, then 1, and Brady found tight end Daniel Graham for a 1-yard score.

Adam Vinatieri added a 40-yard field goal early in the second quarter for a 10-0 lead before the Dolphins came roaring back after a missed Vinatieri field goal from 47 yards gave the Dolphins the ball at their 37. Miami kept the ball on the

ground with Brock Forsey running hard before Fiedler found Chambers to make it 10-7.

That was as close as it would get.

The Patriots got it up to 24-7 early in the second half on a six-play, 48-yard drive that ended with Abdullah's 1-yard run. Dillon's power run down the sideline for 36 yards on third and 2 aided that drive, but he banged up an ankle on the play. He returned for one play in the fourth quarter.

The Dolphins shot themselves in the foot again on that drive with a pass interference call on Morlon Greenwood that gave the Pats a first down at the Miami 1.

The Dolphins had their chances in the fourth quarter, but they reverted to what they've been since Ricky Williams deserted them: a team that can't score to save its life. ◥

DAVID PATTEN WRESTS THE BALL AWAY FROM A PAIR OF DOLPHINS. AT LEFT, TED JOHNSON SOARS OVER MIAMI QUARTERBACK JAY FIEDLER AFTER RODNEY HARRISON'S FOURTH-QUARTER SACK.

COLTS
CARDINALS
BILLS
DOLPHINS
SEAHAWKS
JETS
STEELERS
RAMS
BILLS
CHIEFS
RAVENS
BROWNS
BENGALS
DOLPHINS
JETS
49ERS

BY NICK CAFARDO

Having the final say

30-20

SEA	0	6	3	11
NE	10	10	0	10

10/17/2004
50°, CLOUDY, WINDY
GILLETTE STADIUM
FOXBOROUGH

THE PATRIOTS WON THEIR 20TH GAME in a row, and tied the NFL record for most consecutive regular-season wins (17). Those are feats that take all the emotion the players can muster week after week.

Each week there is a new cause to rally around. Next up would be a matchup against AFC East rival New York, also 5-0, but this week, Rodney Harrison took a few words from usually quiet Seattle receiver Darrell Jackson, who said among other things the Patriots were "beatable," and he turned them into what Harrison called "fuel for the fire."

"Two losses in a row [for the Seahawks]," Harrison said. "Breaks my heart."

The fiery Patriots safety, who had another strong game in the 30-20 win over the Seahawks at Gillette Stadium, said the team plays too hard to accept what he terms "disrespectful chatter" from the opposition. Harrison believes New England's opponents should respect "a bunch of guys who work hard every week to prepare to play football as a team." He claimed he turned to Jackson at one

point and said, "Why don't you just shut up and play?"

"We don't have a bunch of clowns in here," Harrison said. "We have good, quality people. It's a tough locker room if you're a prima donna. There's not one guy who singles himself out as being better or different than anyone else."

If wide receiver Bethel Johnson was in danger of becoming one of those guys, a trip to the Bill Belichick House of Detention seems to have rehabilitated him quickly. Johnson, who according to team sources was having problems executing the plays in the playbook, and was inactive for last week's game, made the catch of his life late in the fourth quarter. His full-extension, diving grab of a 48-yard pass from Tom Brady after outracing everyone in a Seahawk uniform kept alive New England's clinching drive.

"I guarantee that he is definitely the only guy on this team and probably one of the few guys in the league that could have caught up to that ball, because of his speed," said Patriots cornerback Ty Law.

The Seahawks' Josh Brown had just made a 31-yard field goal to trim the Patriots' advantage to 23-20 with 3:01 left. Brown, however, hit a bad kickoff to the 9, and Johnson ran it to the Patriot 37, from where New England started its clinching march.

Johnson's great grab came on third

NEW ENGLAND	FIRST DOWNS	RUSHING YARDS	PASSING YARDS	TURNOVERS
SEATTLE	20/23	138/102	224/341	2/2

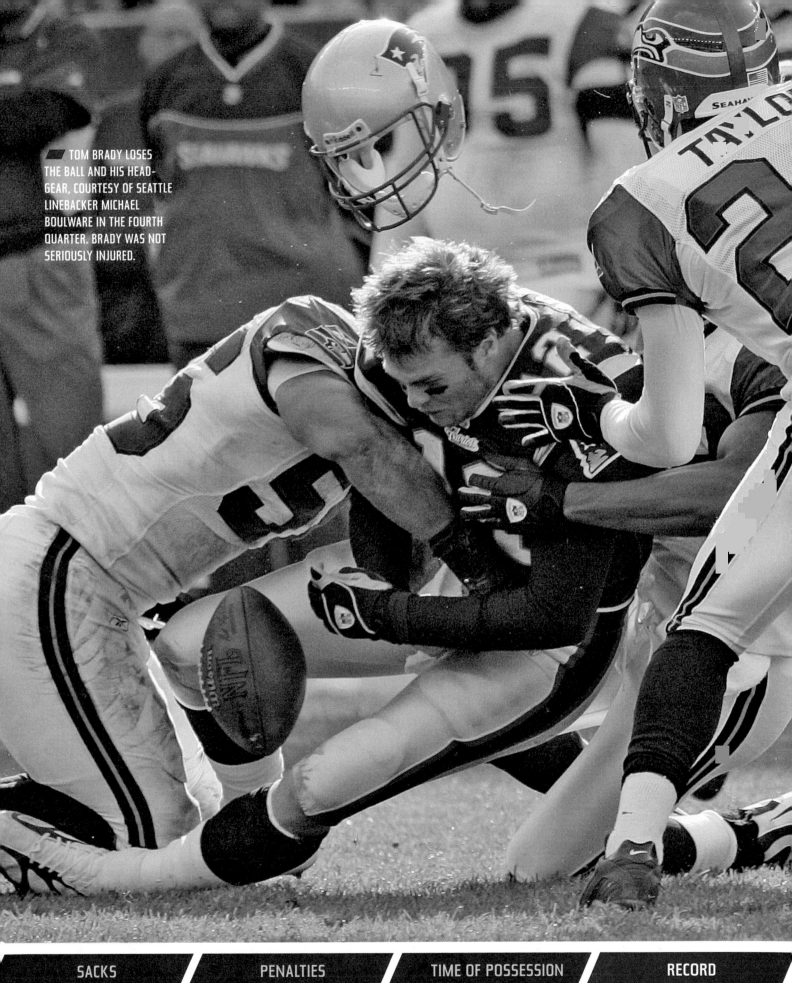

TOM BRADY LOSES THE BALL AND HIS HEADGEAR, COURTESY OF SEATTLE LINEBACKER MICHAEL BOULWARE IN THE FOURTH QUARTER. BRADY WAS NOT SERIOUSLY INJURED.

SACKS	PENALTIES	TIME OF POSSESSION	RECORD
3/1	6-46/6-50	31:37/28:23	5-0/3-2

Clinging to a 23-20 lead, the Patriots faced a third and 7 at their 40 when Tom Brady hit Bethel Johnson on a 48-yard completion to set up the clinching score. The Patriots lined up in the shotgun with Johnson split wide right, David Givens in the left slot and David Patten wide left. TE Daniel Graham was in motion. Brady rolled to his left and Johnson put an inside move on Marcus Trufant and then dusted the second-year cornerback. Meanwhile, Graham helped block defensive end Grant Wistrom before kicking out and chip blocking Chike Okeafor and Michael Boulware, who were bearing down on Brady. The drive was capped by a Corey Dillon 9-yard touchdown run.

and 7 from the Patriot 40. The completion was challenged by Seahawks coach Mike Holmgren, but the call on the field was upheld. While the ball hit the ground with Johnson's arms wrapped around it, the ruling was that the receiver had held on. The play appeared to break the spirits of the Seahawks, who two plays later allowed a 9-yard touchdown run by Corey Dillon, who controlled the clock for the Patriots all day with 105 yards and two touchdowns on 23 carries.

"I think he made a great catch," Holmgren said of Johnson's acrobatics. "I saw the play differently from the referee, but any way you look at it, it was a great effort by a great athlete. But, you know what, that is what this team has been able to do. It's a remarkable thing. You tip your hat to them."

Holmgren had to be fuming about his team's lack of timing. Seattle had only six penalties, but they all seemed to come at the wrong time.

On their next-to-last drive, when they settled for the field goal, the Seahawks had first and 10 at the Patriots 13. They committed two penalties on one play, both of which the Patriots declined. Then Matt Hasselbeck committed intentional grounding on second and 12 from the Patriot 15,

which cost Seattle 10 yards and a loss of down. Before the Seahawks knew it, it was fourth down, and instead of going for 7 points and the lead, they settled for 3 to trail by 3.

Hasselback, the former Boston College signal-caller, went 27 of 50 for 349 yards, no touchdowns, and two interceptions.

Both of his interceptions led to scores in the first quarter. After Richard Seymour tipped a pass, Willie McGinest came down with it and ran 27 yards to the Seahawks 26. Dillon ran it in from the 1 for the Patriots' first score. On the Seahawks' next possession, Law made a nice interception, diving along the sideline in front of Jackson at the Seattle 43.

Brady, who went 19 for 30 for 231 yards, completed a couple of passes to get Adam Vinatieri within field goal range from 40 yards, making it 10-0.

With 12:32 remaining in the second quarter, Brady connected with a wide-open David Patten for a 6-yard TD pass, giving the Patriots a 17-0 lead.

The Patriots were very proud of limiting the Seahawks to the field goal in the red zone during crunch time.

"We tried to keep containment on the quarterback and the coverage was pretty tight down there," Belichick said. "I think those defensive backs stepped up and did a nice job on those receivers."

"The red zone was a point of emphasis all week," Harrison said. "With their offense, and the great players they have over there, they're used to marching down the field and scoring 7 points."

The Seahawks might have won but for the penalties and some drops by their receivers. Part of that was the intimidation of Law and Harrison, but even so Hasselbeck brought Seattle back by engineering drives capped by field goals by Brown, the second of which made it 20-6 at the half. Brown added a 28-yarder in the third quarter.

On the first play of the fourth quarter, in a scary moment, Brady had his helmet ripped off by Michael Boulware and fumbled. The Patriots held off Seattle there, but the next time New England had the ball, Brady, with a lot of time to throw, was picked off by Boulware at the Patriot 45. The Seahawks then pounded home their only touchdown on Shaun Alexander's 9-yard run with 11:05 left in the fourth, and after Hasselbeck connected with tight end Jerramy Stevens for the 2-point conversion, it was 20-17.

The teams traded field goals, leading up to the final three minutes, when the New England defense dominated.

"I'm enjoying this, trust me," a satisfied Harrison said. "All that talk from Seattle all week..."

SEATTLE'S KEN HAMLIN TAKES DOWN PATRIOTS TIGHT END DANIEL GRAHAM AFTER ONE OF GRAHAM'S FOUR RECEPTIONS. THE DRIVE RESULTED IN AN ADAM VINATIERI FIELD GOAL IN THE SECOND QUARTER.

COLTS
CARDINALS
BILLS
DOLPHINS
SEAHAWKS
JETS
STEELERS
RAMS
BILLS
CHIEFS
RAVENS
BROWNS
BENGALS
DOLPHINS
JETS
49ERS

BY NICK CAFARDO

Good enough

13-7

NYJ	0	7	0	0
NE	3	10	0	0

10/24/2004
46°, CLOUDY, WINDY
GILLETTE STADIUM
FOXBOROUGH

AS THE NEWSPAPER OF RECORD, WE must inform our readers that the 13-7 Patriots victory over the New York Jets in Game 6 broke the NFL record for consecutive regular-season victories. The team has 18, 21 overall.

We also had to inform the participants.

"Is that right?" said Patriots wide receiver David Patten, who caught what held up as the winning touchdown pass from Tom Brady from 7 yards out with five seconds remaining in the first half. "I didn't know that. It is what it is. It's a sign we've done a great job to this point, but we have two-thirds of the season to play."

Coach Bill Belichick said that neither before nor after the defensive struggle did he mention the NFL record. In fact, he said, "[I] didn't say one word about it." What meant more than the amazing streak of excellence was that the Patriots took sole possession of first place in the AFC East by beating their divisional rivals, a team that wasn't quite ready to knock the dynasty-in-the-making off its game.

It was another instance of the Patriots

(6-0) doing what they had to do at the most opportune time, just as in so many of their other wins. A team that hates to mention individual accolades got 115 yards on 22 carries from Corey Dillon; five receptions for 107 yards from David Givens, who shouldered the load with Deion Branch and Troy Brown out with injuries; and a 20-for-29 (for 230 yards and one TD) performance from Brady, who had a gaudy 104.1 quarterback rating. New England also gave tremendous effort on defense, holding the Jets to 268 total yards of offense and Curtis Martin to 70 yards on 20 carries.

And like most games during the streak, the opposition had a chance to overtake the Patriots at one time or another. When that time comes, the Patriots, who have asserted themselves as the best late-game team in football, usually make a huge stop or break the opposing team's rhythm.

Such a play occurred on third and 5 from the Patriots' 27 with 2:48 remaining when Martin ran his patented draw play and the Patriots were ready to seize the moment once more.

Richard Seymour pushed the pocket from the right end. Willie McGinest came from the back side and once again made one of his amazing stops, a la the one he made against Indianapolis last season, or the one against Tennessee. He nailed Martin for a 3-yard loss, the same Martin Belichick said during the week never

	FIRST DOWNS		RUSHING YARDS	PASSING YARDS	TURNOVERS
NEW ENGLAND	21/15	NEW YORK	133/106	210/162	1/1

EUGENE WILSON SNAGS RODNEY HARRISON BY THE JERSEY AFTER HARRISON BROKE UP CHAD PENNINGTON'S PASS INTENDED FOR WAYNE CHREBET. THE FOURTH-DOWN PLAY SNUFFED OUT THE JETS' FINAL CHANCE.

SACKS	PENALTIES	TIME OF POSSESSION	RECORD
0/3	6-53/6-37	28:59/31:01	6-0/5-1

NEW ENGLAND'S RICHARD SEYMOUR (93) AND TEDY BRUSCHI ZERO IN ON THE JETS' CURTIS MARTIN.

makes negative plays. Until that moment, he had not.

"In that situation, you have to play the run first," McGinest said. "I had my half and Richard had his half and we came together and made a play."

It wasn't the final play for the Jets (5-1), either, but the Patriots took care of that as

well. On fourth and 8, Chad Pennington threw downfield to Wayne Chrebet. The veteran slot receiver was covered well all day by free agent rookie Randall Gay, and he once again was all over Chrebet. The Patriots figured Pennington would look for Chrebet on such an important throw and Rodney Harrison came over to break

panic. Someone always steps up and makes a play."

The Jets rebounded from a 6-0 deficit with a touchdown with 1:55 to go before halftime. The score capped a 13-play, 78-yard drive, 23 of which came on Martin's running (he surpassed Jim Brown for seventh on the all-time rushing list). Pennington, who went 6 for 6 on the drive, kept the ball for the 1-yard score.

That's normally enough time for the Patriots to recover. And they did.

After Bethel Johnson's 28-yard return, which let the Patriots start the drive at their 38, Brady went into his two-minute offense, tossing to Johnson for 14, Kevin Faulk over the middle for 24, Faulk for 5 more, and Patten for 11. The Jets' Dewayne Robertson then was flagged for roughing the passer, which placed the ball at the 7.

Brady stepped up in the pocket and found Patten in the back of the end zone for the score to give the Patriots a 13-7 halftime lead.

"I always expect he's going to find me," Patten said of Brady. "That kid is unbelievable. The tight end ran a hook route and I think took the safety over with him and that left me free at the back of the end zone and Tom never misses us when we're out there."

The Jets entered the game as the least penalized team in the league and had the third-best turnover ratio. One turnover and six penalties killed them.

The Patriots got a 41-yard field goal by Adam Vinatieri with 8:33 remaining in the first quarter, and a 27-yarder with 9:31 remaining in the second quarter.

There was a third-quarter lull as both teams had extended drives that didn't lead to anything until Corey Dillon sprang up the middle on a nice lead block by guard Stephen Neal and raced 44 yards to the Jets' 41.

The Jets caught a break when John Abraham leveled Dan Klecko on a pass reception, which caused a fumble, and left Klecko writhing with a leg injury.

The ball was recovered by Eric Barton at the Jets 39, but the Patriots' defense forced a punt.

At that point Dillon, who was the first 100-yard rusher the Jets had allowed this season, began icing the game for the Patriots. ◀

up the play, preserving the victory.

"We knew [Chrebet] was getting the ball all along," said Harrison. "He's a fantastic receiver."

The Patriots have concentration, maturity, "and we don't panic," Harrison said. "We go through a lot of situational football, so when it is a critical moment, we don't

PLAY OF THE
GAME

:05

2ND QUARTER

Trailing, 7-6, the Patriots had a second down at the Jets' 7-yard line with 11 seconds left in the first half, moments after a roughing-the-passer call on Dewayne Robertson. With the Jets pressuring from the outside, Tom Brady moved up in the pocket and passed on the run from the 10-yard line, finding David Patten. Patten had lined up wide right and was running along the back of the end zone, beating Terrell Buckley for the touchdown.

BY NICK CAFARDO

Busted at 21

34-20

NE	3	7	3	7
PIT	21	3	10	0

10/31/2004
64°, FAIR
HEINZ FIELD
PITTSBURGH

THEIR BASEBALL BROTHERS, THE RED Sox, are proof that all streaks must end, winning the World Series after an 86-year drought. So as if to balance the slate, the sports gods looked down upon New England and said, "Do not be greedy."

Thus, the Patriots' record 21-game winning streak ended. The Team That Could Not Lose finally met its match in the Pittsburgh Steelers, 34-20, before a record-breaking Heinz Field crowd of 64,737.

There were no excuses from anyone in the Patriots locker room as to why they lost for the first time since Sept. 28, 2003, to the Steve Spurrier-coached Washington Redskins.

That's because the Steelers played very much in their tradition, dominating the trenches, creating mistakes, and smashing Patriots quarterback Tom Brady in the mouth every chance they got.

"I wish we could play again tomorrow," said New England defensive end Willie McGinest. "We're not going to make any excuses, like blame the refs, or injuries, or anything like that. It's disappointing we

got our butts kicked and got outplayed. We have to come in tomorrow and look in the mirror and make sure each and every one of us can see what we did to add to this. It's not the end of the world. We have time to come back from this."

The Steelers forced turnovers — four of them — which led to Pittsburgh scores. Two were caused by linebacker Jerry Porter, who played an emotional game, saying he was fired up by words McGinest uttered to him before the opening kickoff.

If that was the case he made the Patriots pay big time, and young quarterback Ben Roethlisberger (18 for 24 for 196 yards, two touchdowns and a 126.4 rating) looked as calm and collected as a guy named Bradshaw in picking apart the wounded Patriots secondary.

They didn't make excuses, but the Patriots were missing starting running back Corey Dillon, had to use a makeshift offensive line with starting right tackle Tom Ashworth out with a back ailment, and then lost left tackle Matt Light, who got the wind knocked out of him.

The Patriots also lost cornerback Ty Law to a foot injury in the third series of the game, and the Steelers went right at rookie free agent Randall Gay and made the Patriots pay.

But in the past, the Patriots had never missed a beat because of injuries.

"We've lost players to injuries before," said linebacker Tedy Bruschi. "We play

NEW ENGLAND	FIRST DOWNS	PITTSBURGH	RUSHING YARDS	PASSING YARDS	TURNOVERS
	19/25		5/221	243/196	4/0

THE STEELERS SEEEMED TO MAKE ALL THE PLAYS, INCLUDING IKE TAYLOR'S SECOND-QUARTER INTERCEPTION OF A TOM BRADY PASS INTENDED FOR BETHEL JOHNSON.

SACKS	PENALTIES	TIME OF POSSESSION	RECORD
0/4	6-55/9-90	17:02/42:58	6-1/6-1

PATRIOTS COACH BILL BELICHICK HAD SEEN ENOUGH, AND IT WASN'T EVEN HALFTIME.

AFTER 21 CONSECUTIVE VICTORIES, THE PATRIOTS AND QUARTERBACK TOM BRADY WERE OUT OF ANSWERS.

ADDING INJURY TO INSULT, PATRIOTS CORNERBACK TY LAW WAS HELPED OFF THE FIELD WITH A FOOT INJURY THAT ENDED UP SIDELINING HIM FOR THE SEASON.

as a team. Whoever is in the game has to do their part. That's the way we do it around here."

With Dillon out, New England ran the ball six times for 5 yards, forcing Brady to throw it 43 times. The defense allowed the Steelers to romp for 221 yards on 49 carries, 125 of them from Duce Staley on 25 carries. Jerome Bettis, who ran for 65 more yards on 15 carries after totaling 64 yards in the first six games, was effective in the fourth quarter.

Time of possession was 42:58 to 17:02 in favor of the Steelers, who amassed 417 yards in total offense to the Patriots' 248.

Would things have been different if Dillon or Law had played?

"I couldn't forecast how [Dillon] was going to play," said Brady, who threw for 271 yards but was picked off twice and sacked four times. "Corey's absence didn't force me into fumbling the ball."

No curses or outside forces at work here. Just a plain old "butt-whipping" as linebacker Mike Vrabel would call it.

Dexter Reid had a chance to pin the Steelers inside the 5-yard line on a punt early in the first quarter, but instead, Josh Miller's booming punt trickled into the end zone for a touchback.

It was a big break for the Steelers, who converted their first touchdown on the same series when Law turned the wrong way on coverage of Hines Ward and went down in a heap.

Two plays later, Roethlisberger tossed a 47-yard bomb to Plaxico Burress over Gay, who was in one-on-one coverage. The touchdown, with 3:46 remaining in the first, gave the Steelers a 7-3 lead they would not relinquish.

"It was an all-out blitz," said Roethlisberger. "You have to give the line a lot of credit, because there shouldn't have been time like that. I saw Plaxico running with a guy on him and I just tried to throw it as far as I could."

Porter wreaked havoc on Brady on the Patriots' next possession, blitzing, sacking Brady, and forcing the ball loose at the Patriots' 27.

After four runs by Staley, Roethlisberger found Burress in the end zone from 4 yards out over Eugene Wilson. The Patriots challenged the diving sideline catch, but it was upheld. Just like that, it was 14-3, and the bad times just wouldn't end.

Brady's first play of the next series wound up in the hands of right corner Deshea Townsend, who stepped in front of Bethel Johnson, who had slipped, and took off down the right sideline. His 39-yard score with 13 seconds left in the first made it 21-3.

"They all hurt," said coach Bill Belichick of the turnovers. "Seven hurt, 14 hurt, 21 hurt. 14-3 would have been more manageable than 21-3. When we turn the ball over and we can't stop them on top of that, we're dead."

But after winning 21 straight, this team never seems dead.

Sure, Brady threw another pick on a long pass intended for Johnson in the second quarter, and that led to a 19-yard field goal by Jeff Reed with 2:06 left in the half, upping the ante to 24-3. But the Steelers committed a big no-no before the end of the half. Playing in a prevent defense, they allowed Brady to put up a touchdown in a two-minute offense, his 2-yard pass finding David

Givens with 42 seconds remaining.

That momentum just didn't carry over.

In fact, Porter created what might have been the biggest turnover of all in the third quarter. He hit Kevin Faulk so hard on a dump-off pass, that Faulk coughed up the ball at the Patriot 17.

The Steelers scored four plays later, with Bettis getting into the end zone for the eighth time this season on a 2-yard run with 13:06 left in the third to make it 31-10. ◄

:13

1ST QUARTER

Trailing 14-3, and with the first quarter winding down, the Patriots come out with a five-receiver set on first down at their 33. The decision proves costly when Brady has to rush his throw, which results in an interception that cornerback Deshea Townsend returns 39 yards for a score, breaking the game open.

COLTS
CARDINALS
BILLS
DOLPHINS
SEAHAWKS
JETS
STEELERS
RAMS
BILLS
CHIEFS
RAVENS
BROWNS
BENGALS
DOLPHINS
JETS
49ERS

BY RON BORGES

Be prepared

40-22

NE	6	13	14	7
STL	0	14	0	8

11/7/2004
INDOORS
EDWARD JONES DOME
ST. LOUIS

OVER THE LAST THREE YEARS, THE New England Patriots have defined the word "team." On this day, they redefined it and along the way embarrassed an ill-prepared team that couldn't execute, the St. Louis Rams, 40-22, at the Edward Jones Dome.

The Patriots had a linebacker catch a pass for a touchdown, a kicker throw a pass for a touchdown, and a wide receiver, practice squad player, linebacker, and rookie free agent all play defensive back at various times without serious consequences. It all symbolized what has made the Patriots the most resilient team in the league.

"This is probably as much of a team victory as anything I've ever been around," coach Bill Belichick said. "They fought to the end. That's what a team's about. Everyone doing their job."

With both starting cornerbacks and right tackle Tom Ashworth out before the opening kickoff, and reserve corner Asante Samuel knocked out for much of the day on the Rams' second play with a jammed shoulder, the Patriots were facing the kind of uphill battle to which Sisyphus could have related.

But that ancient myth did not apply in the end because the Patriots not only pushed their personal boulder up the hill but then rolled it over the Rams.

Always, it seems, these Patriots play their best when the situation is at its worst, and it couldn't get much worse than having their secondary riddled by injury as they were facing one of the most explosive pass offenses in football.

Despite those problems, they left their opponent so bamboozled that after three quarters the Rams had attempted only 19 passes. If ever there was a game that cried out for abandoning a sense of balance, this was it. But St. Louis failed to take that course in part because the Patriots were hellbent on harassing their quarterback, sacking Marc Bulger five times and knocking him around on many other occasions.

Meanwhile, the Rams committed enough turnovers (three) and penalties (10) to beat themselves.

"I think it really came down to being more physical than they were," defensive end Richard Seymour said. "We wanted to pressure Bulger to get the ball out of there quick so they didn't have time to get into their routes."

New England's secondary problems were compounded on the second defensive play of the game when Samuel injured his right shoulder tackling tight end Brandon Manumaleuna. Samuel was replaced by wide receiver Troy Brown, who was in-

NEW ENGLAND	FIRST DOWNS	ST. LOUIS	RUSHING YARDS	PASSING YARDS	TURNOVERS
	22/21		147/81	229/259	1/3

volved in a tackle on running back Marshall Faulk on the very next play. Before the day was out, Brown would be the epitome of what the Patriots are about, catching a touchdown pass on a fake field goal, making three receptions, three tackles, and nearly intercepting two passes.

"The coaches were schooling me on the run," Brown said of his first NFL game as the Chuck Bednarik of his day, a two-way player in a time of specialists. "It was a little intimidating at first to be out there against some of the best guys to play wide receiver, but after I got a little sweat worked up I got more comfortable. That's what they teach you around here. Prepare for everything."

While the Patriots were prepared for everything, the Rams seemed prepared for nothing. By the end of the third quarter they trailed, 33-14, yet had thrown the ball only three more times than they had run it, a fact that dumbfounded many of the Patriots' defenders.

"I thought they'd take more shots downfield," safety Rodney Harrison admitted. "I figured they'd air it out, air it out, air it out. That's what their fans figured, too, the way they were booing [them]. That's what everyone was anticipating. We weren't doing anything fancy. Everyone was just lining up and doing their job."

After two Adam Vinatieri field goals gave the Patriots a 6-0 first-quarter lead, St. Louis struck back, but not by taking advantage of New England's defense. Instead the Rams hammered Tom Brady in the end zone when offensive coordinator Charlie Weis unwisely decided to throw from the 6-yard line to open the second quarter.

Defensive tackle Damione Lewis pushed guard Joe Andruzzi back into the pocket, then reached over him and grabbed Brady's right arm as he tried to throw, knocking the ball loose. Defensive end Leonard Little fell on it and the Rams held a 7-6 lead without the St. Louis offense having done a thing.

In typical Patriot fashion, Brady led his team back down the field immediately, moving it 64 yards in 10 plays to take the lead

SACKS	PENALTIES	TIME OF POSSESSION	RECORD
5/2	7-48/10-80	31:45/28:15	7-1/4-4

TROY BROWN CAUGHT THE RAMS NAPPING FOR A KEY TOUCHDOWN IN THE THIRD QUARTER.

back. Staying with the theme of all hands on deck, linebacker Mike Vrabel made a fingertip catch and tiptoed to keep his feet in bounds in the corner of the end zone for a 2-yard score that made it 13-7.

St. Louis coach Mike Martz seemed to finally notice the battered nature of the Patriots' secondary and went after it as soon as the Rams got the ball back. The big play was a 48-yard throw to Manumaleuna on a seam route on which he beat a linebacker with no apparent safety help behind him. Manumaleuna legged the ball to the 11-yard line and Bulger got the rest of it on the next play when he found Isaac Bruce wide open on a shallow cross for a touchdown that put the Rams back ahead, 14-13, with 5:19 left in the half.

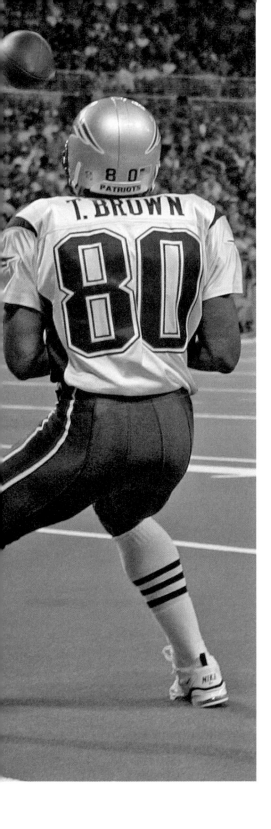

yarder, and it was 16-14.

St. Louis got the ensuing kickoff and shredded New England's Cover-2 defense, completing throws of 15 and 22 yards to Torry Holt with poor Earthwind Moreland, who was activated off the practice squad only two days before, looking for help. He got it, but the Rams still needed only two plays to move the ball from their 34 to the New England 29 with two minutes left in the half. The defense came through at that point, hitting Bulger as he rolled left on the next play, knocking the ball loose. As it rolled toward the sideline, Jarvis Green dived on it at the Patriots 28.

One play later, Little was called for roughing the passer and the crowd grew surly. Despite the deafening booing, Brady calmly completed a 20-yard throw to David Patten on third and 10 to the Rams' 37 with 37 seconds to play and another throw under pressure for 19 yards to Patten to set up Vinatieri's fourth field goal, a 36-yarder, as time ran out to make it 19-14 New England.

Things only got more embarrassing for the Rams in the second half. Once again Vinatieri was involved when he took a direct snap after lining up for an apparent 21-yard field goal try, and instead threw a pass to a wide-open Brown. By the time the Rams noticed Brown, he was standing all alone near the sideline and it was too late to do anything about it but point fingers.

"I was trying to get the call to see which field goal block we were going to do," Lewis said. "Next thing you know the ball was in the end zone."

Now trailing, 26-14, the Rams were reeling. Soon they would be completely undone.

Just four plays after Vinatieri's sneak attack, linebacker Willie McGinest was covering the speedy Holt like a blanket and deflected a Bulger pass away. Roman Phifer picked it out of the air and returned it to the Rams' 21.

Barely two minutes later, it was 33-14 after Corey Dillon deked safety Rich Coady out of a shoe and sprinted into the end zone untouched with 3:36 to play in a third quarter that had become an embarrassment for the Rams.

"I don't know why we continue not to play to our capabilities," Rams safety Adam Archuleta said.

Maybe because yesterday they were playing a team that always plays to its capabilities. And sometimes beyond them. ◄

Barely two minutes later, the Patriots had the lead back when Brady lofted a perfect throw to David Givens for a 50-yard reception on which cornerback Jerametrius Butler had equally perfect coverage and still was scorched by the combination of a beautiful throw and tremendous catch. Although New England's offense stalled at that point, Vinatieri delivered his third field goal, a 45-

Ahead, 19-14, midway through the third quarter, the Patriots were faced with a fourth-and-goal at the Rams' 4-yard line. They sent out kicker Adam Vinatieri ostensibly to attempt his fifth field goal of the game. However, wide receiver Troy Brown came on the field for the play, getting as far as the numbers. He didn't go into the huddle, though, and wandered back toward the sideline. Instead of snapping the ball to holder Josh Miller, the ball went directly to Vinateri. He turned to his left and threw to Brown, left, who was uncovered and walked into the end zone.

BY NICK CAFARDO

Home rule

29-6

BUF	0	0	6	0
NE	3	17	3	6

11/14/2004
40°, CLEAR
GILLETTE STADIUM
FOXBOROUGH

IF YOU LISTENED TO PATRIOTS COACH Bill Belichick and others speaking about the Bills coming into this game, Drew Bledsoe was playing like the second coming of Johnny Unitas, and Willis McGahee was running like Walter Payton.

At the conclusion of 60 minutes of football though, Bledsoe looked more like a 40-something George Blanda while McGahee looked like a running back with a bad leg.

By virtue of a 29-6 win over the Bills at Gillette Stadium, the Patriots kept pace with the Pittsburgh Steelers for the best record in the AFC at 8-1. They also went two games up on the New York Jets in the East Division.

The "new-look" Bills never materialized as the Patriots scorched them with touchdown passes by Tom Brady to David Patten for 13 yards and Christian Fauria for 5, Corey Dillon's fifth 100-yard rushing game (151 yards), and Adam Vinatieri's five field goals.

"We didn't play well enough to beat anybody," lamented Bills coach Mike

Mularkey. "They don't make any mistakes. I felt like all week I got caught up in the fact that we felt good about the week we had. The players were excited about it. I wish I had an answer. They challenged us to bring it at them and we didn't answer the call."

Bledsoe, 8 for 19 for 76 yards and a quarterback rating of 14.3 in one of his worst games as a pro, was continually pressured and forced into bad throws after the Patriots had stopped McGahee (14 carries for 37 yards) in his tracks. Bledsoe was picked off three times, and the ultimate indignity was getting intercepted by Troy Brown in the fourth quarter on a pass intended for Eric Moulds.

"Eric Moulds was in the slot and he's their go-to guy," said Brown, who caught many passes from Bledsoe when he was the Patriots' QB. "I figured they'd be throwing it to him, so I was ready."

The only positive for the Bills, who had only eight first downs, converted no third downs in seven attempts, and were outgained in net yards, 428-125, was a 70-yard punt return in the third quarter by Jonathan Smith, which ruined New England's shutout bid.

Bledsoe was trying to shed the image that he can't play well against New England. He now has a 1-5 record against his former team.

Bledsoe has thrown 11 interceptions and five touchdown passes in games

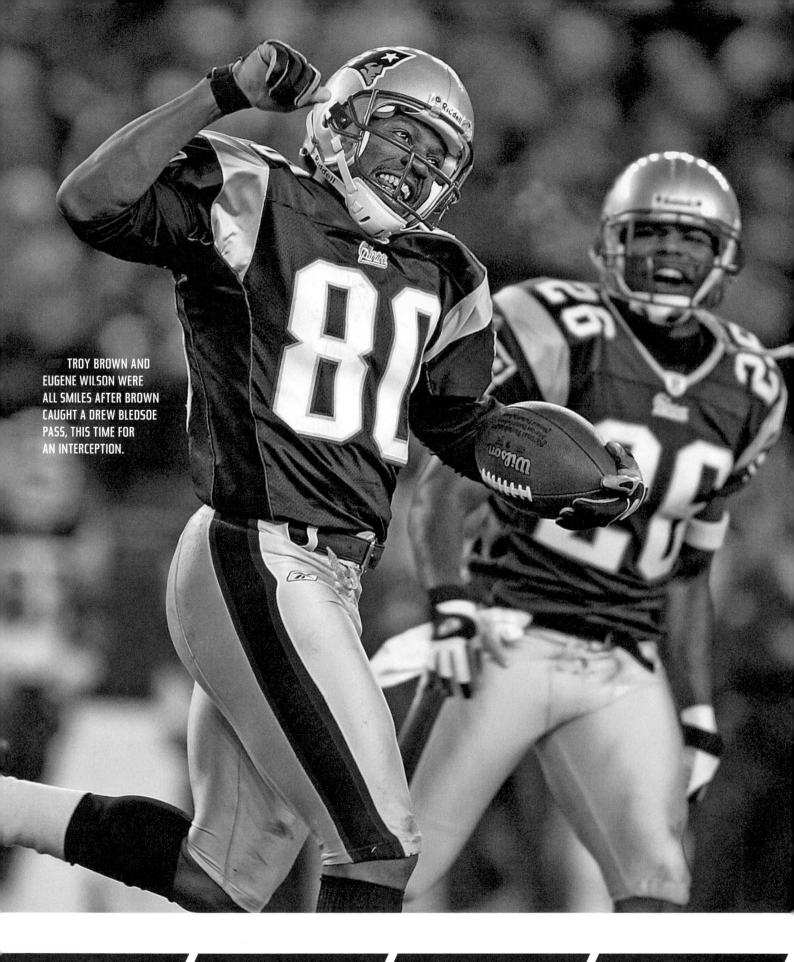

TROY BROWN AND EUGENE WILSON WERE ALL SMILES AFTER BROWN CAUGHT A DREW BLEDSOE PASS, THIS TIME FOR AN INTERCEPTION.

SACKS	PENALTIES	TIME OF POSSESSION	RECORD
3/2	5-44/2-48	41:22/18:38	8-1/3-6

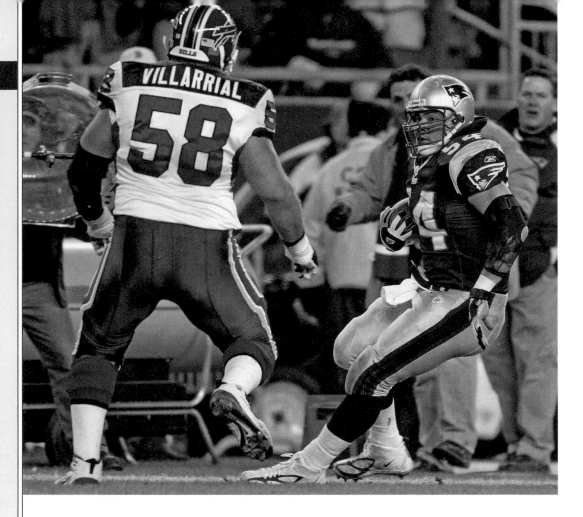

2:24
2ND QUARTER

Down 13-0, with 2:24 left in the second quarter, Buffalo had a chance to get back into the game if it could score before halftime. The Bills lined up at their 45 with Willis McGahee as the lone back and sent rookie receiver Lee Evans in motion left to right. At the snap, Evans took off on a curl route. Then Patriots LB Tedy Bruschi backpedaled into coverage, keeping his eyes on Bills QB Drew Bledsoe, who unleashed a strike toward Evans. However, Bruschi stepped in front of the pass, right, and intercepted it at the New England 44.

against Belichick's team. Brady is now 7-1 against Buffalo, throwing 14 touchdown passes and seven interceptions against the Bills.

While the Patriots settled for 3 points in their first two red zone visits, they managed two touchdowns in their next two, taking a 20-0 halftime lead.

"It seemed as if we were dominating the game, but we'd only come up with 3 points," said Fauria. "We kept saying, 'We should be up by more than 6-0.' "

The first second-quarter drive went 75 yards, Brady finishing it with a 13-yard pass to Patten in the back of the end zone with 3:56 remaining in the half after Rashad Baker had fallen, leaving Patten alone.

"I ran a post route and [Brady] threw me the ball. That was a major catch for us," said Patten.

Bledsoe then tossed his second interception, to Tedy Bruschi in the middle of the field.

The linebacker ran the pass intended for receiver Lee Evans back 29 yards to the Bills' 27. Four plays later, Brady

found Fauria for a 5-yard score with 35 seconds remaining in the half.

"It was just one of those routes where I was in blocking and then slipped out into an open space where I could [catch] the ball," said Fauria.

The best the Bills looked offensively was on their first possession, when they made three first downs, but then they had to punt.

When the Patriots took over, Corey Dillon had six carries good for 43 yards, the big one a 30-yard burst from the Patriot 20 to midfield on first down. The Patriots settled for a 27-yard field goal by Vinatieri.

It marked the 17th straight game the Patriots had scored first.

The Bills were trying to sustain the power running game McGahee had given them the previous three weeks, but it was clear the Patriots were keying on the second-year back, making Bledsoe throw it to beat them.

"We were determined not to let [McGahee] gain 100 yards on us," said safety Rodney Harrison. "It was huge that we stopped him, and it really gave us a chance to dictate the game."

Bledsoe was able to connect on midrange passes, but when he tried to exploit the banged-up Patriots secondary deep he was picked off by Eugene Wilson on the final play of the first quarter at the Patriots 3.

The Patriots drove downfield, including some more hard running by Dillon, who busted loose for gains of 13 and 19 yards. Brady also hit Bethel Johnson on the fly over the middle for a 47-yard gain to the Buffalo 26.

The Bills' defense tightened, though, forcing the Patriots to settle for a 24-yard field goal by Vinatieri, making it a 6-0 Patriots lead with 10:35 remaining in the second quarter.

The competitiveness of the game had ended long before the teams took the field in the second half.

By the fourth quarter, many fans had departed, heading down Route 1 in their cars quite confident of the result and equally confident there was nothing the Bills could do. ◄

PATRIOT DEFENDERS JARVIS GREEN AND WILLIE MCGINEST SWARM BILLS QUARTERBACK J.P. LOSMAN, FORCING A FOURTH-QUARTER TURNOVER. ROMAN PHIFER RECOVERED THE FUMBLE.

BY NICK CAFARDO

Run down

27-19

NE	7	10	7	3
KC	10	0	3	6

11/22/2004
45°, OVERCAST
**ARROWHEAD
STADIUM**
KANSAS CITY

THE SWEAT WAS DRIPPING OFF TED Johnson's face as if someone had forgotten to turn off a bathroom faucet. With each drop came the satisfaction that the Patriots' defense again had risen to the challenge, not only holding the No. 1 rushing team in the NFL to 64 yards on the ground and surviving a patchwork secondary for one more week, but holding up in the fourth quarter, allowing the Patriots to claim their ninth win in 10 games this season.

"Our defensive line did an unbelievable job," said Johnson following the 27-19 win over the Chiefs. "We didn't give up anything up the middle. To be a good defense, you have to stop the run. We knew we had to stop their run, and doing that we made them be a one-dimensional team — and that wasn't easy, either."

The Chiefs and their All-Pro offensive line fell far short in the battle of the trenches. Not only was Priest Holmes replacement Derrick Blaylock ineffective inside, but by the time he was able to run well outside, it was time to pass. And de-

spite throwing for 381 yards, Trent Green's night wasn't as impressive as that sounds. He threw a key interception to Rodney Harrison in the end zone before the end of the first half on a ball intended for Tony Gonzalez, which greatly contributed to Kansas City's loss.

Chiefs receivers dropped two passes that could have been scores, one in the first half by Eddie Kennison and another by Johnnie Morton in the second half, while the Patriots received a huge boost with the return of Deion Branch, who caught six passes for 105 yards and a touchdown. Daniel Graham also came up huge with three catches for 83 yards, including a 48-yarder that set the stage for

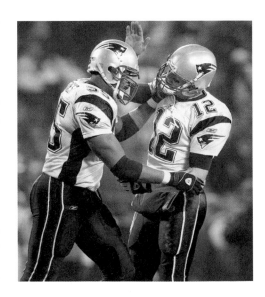

	FIRST DOWNS		RUSHING YARDS	PASSING YARDS	TURNOVERS
NEW ENGLAND	21/20	KANSAS CITY	98/64	309/353	1/1

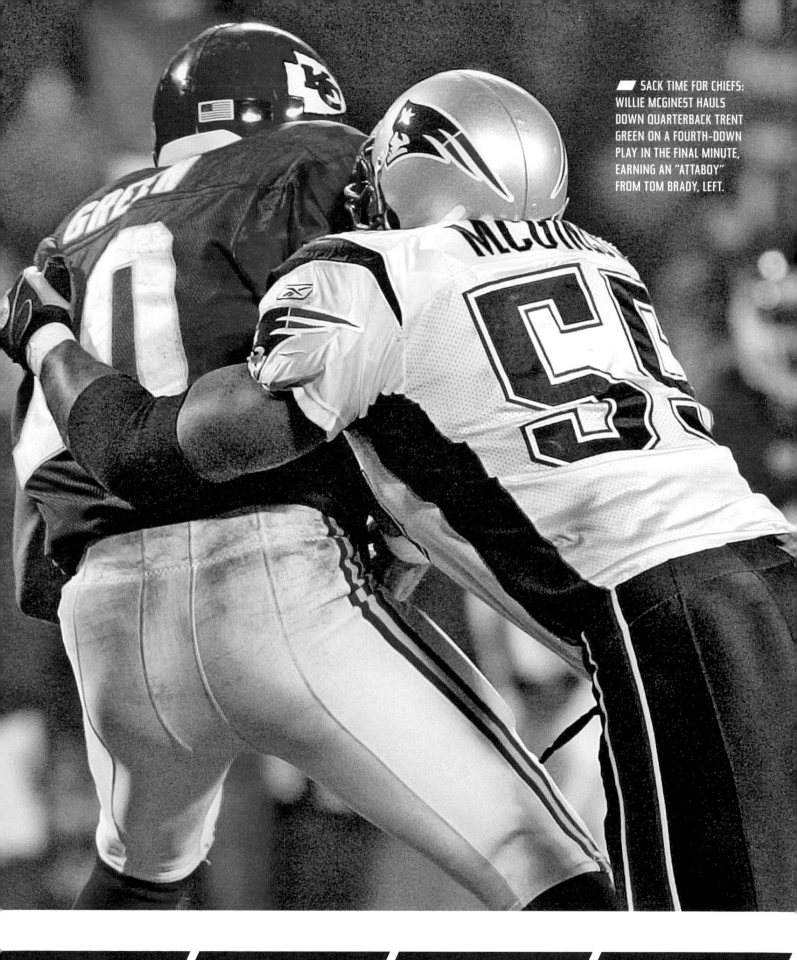

■ SACK TIME FOR CHIEFS: WILLIE MCGINEST HAULS DOWN QUARTERBACK TRENT GREEN ON A FOURTH-DOWN PLAY IN THE FINAL MINUTE, EARNING AN "ATTABOY" FROM TOM BRADY, LEFT.

SACKS	PENALTIES	TIME OF POSSESSION	RECORD
4/1	4-25/7-50	27:59/32:01	9-1/3-7

After Kansas City had closed to within 17-13, the Patriots had a first down at the Chiefs' 26 with 5:03 left in the third quarter. Deion Branch, right, turned a short Tom Brady pass into a touchdown, which proved to be the decisive score. Branch lined up in the slot inside David Patten. Chiefs cornerback William Bartee blitzed, and linebacker Kawika Mitchell came over to cover Branch. Branch then caught a short pass from Brady and cut across the middle, evading Mitchell and linebacker Scott Fujita. Branch then turned upfield, getting a key block from Troy Brown on safety Greg Wesley and beating Fujita and cornerback Eric Warfield to the end zone.

Adam Vinatieri's 37-yard field goal in the second quarter.

Chiefs fans were seeing red because they knew an opportunity to turn their season around had gone by the boards.

Green managed to make a game of it by connecting on a 26-yard touchdown pass to Kennison with 6:13 remaining (though the 2-point conversion failed). The Chiefs marched 97 yards in 11 plays after the defense forced a Corey Dillon fumble at the Kansas City 3. But the Patriots got the ball back and ate up the clock behind Dillon, who fell 2 yards short of 100 and just as many short of 1,000 yards for the season. The Chiefs' D couldn't make a play to pre-vent Vinatieri's field goal with 1:46 left to play, which gave the Pats an 8-point lead.

"I'm disgusted," said Dillon of his fumble. "I was just trying too hard to make things happen. Immediately after that the team told me, 'We need you to come through, run the ball hard, and get us down there.' That's what I did."

The Patriots received a huge defensive game from Ty Warren (seven tackles, two sacks), who seemed to be in the middle of the action most of the night. The downer was that the young and patchwork secondary got burned. Earthwind Moreland was beaten twice for touchdowns and Randall Gay was also beaten downfield.

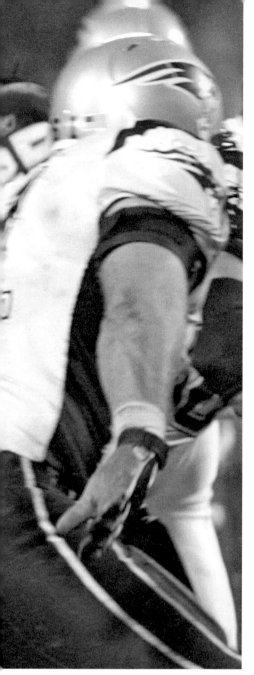

24-yard field goal with 6:45 remaining after the Chiefs had marched from their 27 to the Patriots 5. They were unable to get the six when Tedy Bruschi made a huge play, stuffing Blaylock for a 1-yard loss on third and 1.

Also during that drive, Morton dropped what appeared to be six points on a long pass that hit him between the numbers after he'd beaten Gay. The Patriots' offense, on the other hand, didn't have much difficulty finishing off drives. Tom Brady, who had missed on a long pass to David Patten down the right sideline, went back to it two plays later and connected with Patten over Chiefs nickel back Julian Battles for 46 yards.

On the next play, Brady got the ball out quickly on the left to Branch, who zigged-zagged his way 26 yards into the end zone, getting away from some poor tackle attempts by linebacker Kawika Mitchell and safety Greg Wesley.

That gave the Patriots a 24-13 lead with less than 5 minutes remaining in the third quarter.

"I had the opportunity to make some big plays," said Branch, who had been out with a knee injury. "I think everything worked out well today. It feels real good."

The Patriots silenced the crowd on their first possession, tying a record held by the Miami Dolphins for scoring first in 18 consecutive games. New England took the opening kickoff to its 29 and marched 71 yards in 10 plays, the drive culminating in a 5-yard run by Dillon. ✒

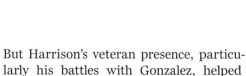

But Harrison's veteran presence, particularly his battles with Gonzalez, helped give the Patriots just enough control.

Harrison said of his interception, "I knew it was coming to Tony. He's the best tight end in the league and he gets the ball in the red zone. I was just reading the quarterback and I was able to get a break on the ball."

The Chiefs got the ball with 1:46 remaining in the game, but Green was unable to pull off any heroics as Willie McGinest sacked him for a 10-yard loss on fourth down with 56 seconds remaining.

The Chiefs got as close as 17-13 in the third quarter when Lawrence Tynes hit a

◼ NEW ENGLAND'S TY WARREN POPS THE BALL OUT OF CHIEFS' QB TRENT GREEN'S HANDS FOR ONE OF HIS TWO SACKS ON THE NIGHT. GREEN RECOVERED THE BALL.

BY NICK CAFARDO

The defense

24-3

BAL	0	3	0	0
NE	0	3	6	15

11/28/2004
52°, RAIN
**GILLETTE
STADIUM**
FOXBOROUGH

BY THE END OF THE 24-3 PATRIOTS win over the Baltimore Ravens in Game 11, the Patriots didn't know whether to sack Kyle Boller or to hug him.

If ever the mercy rule should have applied in the last 10 minutes of a professional football game, this was the time. Boller, the second-year quarterback from Cal, was stripped of the ball, and of his dignity, in the fourth quarter when the Patriots' Jarvis Green fell on a loose ball knocked away from Boller by Tedy Bruschi for the final score of the game.

Boller's jersey and body were covered with mud, blood, and slop in one of the more intense muggings the Patriots have handed a quarterback this season, though the four sacks the defense got credit for didn't do the beating justice.

Boller went 15 for 35 for 93 yards, with one interception and a 38.4 rating.

"He'd had a pretty good run and had been very effective," said Patriots linebacker Rosevelt Colvin of Boller. "We

	FIRST DOWNS		RUSHING YARDS	PASSING YARDS	TURNOVERS
NEW ENGLAND	18/8	BALTIMORE	144/77	170/47	0/2

dominates

TEDY BRUSCHI MAKES AN EMPHATIC POINT AFTER JE'ROD CHERRY DOWNED A JOSH MILLER PUNT AT THE RAVENS' 3-YARD LINE HALFWAY THROUGH THE FOURTH QUARTER

SACKS	PENALTIES	TIME OF POSSESSION	RECORD
4/1	10-97/10-106	35:54/24:06	10-1/7-4

TEDY BRUSCHI POPS THE BALL OUT OF RAVENS QB KYLE BOLLER'S HANDS. JARVIS GREEN FELL ON IT FOR A CLINCHING TOUCHDOWN.

managed to keep control of him. If you can stop the run, then it makes any team one-dimensional, and that's what we were hoping for."

Boller said, "You want to take the dinks and dunks, but at some point you have to go deep in a game like that, and they just did a great job of protecting that."

While at halftime it was 3-3 and a defensive struggle, by the fourth quarter it was raining points — for the Patriots. New England tacked on 21 unanswered points in the second half.

Adam Vinatieri made three field goals during a rainy, windy day at Gillette Stadium, where the Patriots won their 17th straight. New England improved to 10-1 this season.

Heading into December, the only winning team on the schedule is the New York Jets, which bodes well for what might be the best regular season in Patriots history.

There were no surprises in this one.

The Ravens defense didn't allow the Patriots a touchdown until three seconds into the fourth quarter, but the Patriots were able to control the ball on the ground with Corey Dillon surpassing the 1,000-yard mark with 123 yards on 30 carries.

It was only the third time a team had surpassed 100 yards rushing against the Ravens this season, and it was just the second time Dillon had run for 100 yards or more against Ray Lewis in 11 meetings against the All-Pro middle linebacker.

Though Boller hung in there for parts of three quarters, he eventually succumbed on the Bruschi strip.

"Vrabes had him," said Bruschi, referring to linebacker Mike Vrabel. "He managed to slip away, and I was able to sack him and strip the ball from him. Then it was a case of following the ball and trying to get in there, and Jarvis was able to fall on it in the end zone."

Such symmetry, as the Patriots got one defensive score, one offensive score, and 9 points from field goals. The special teams didn't allow a kick return of longer than 28 yards, or a punt return of more than 12.

The defense held the Ravens to 124 net yards and only eight first downs, three of them on the ground. The Patriots held Chester Taylor, playing in place of the injured Jamal Lewis, to 61 yards on 16 carries. It was a unit once again playing without its top three cornerbacks — Ty Law, Tyrone Poole, and Asante Samuel — forcing free safety Eugene Wilson to move to corner. Randall Gay, who picked off his second pass of the season, was at the other corner, and a combination of Wilson, Dexter Reid, Rodney Harrison, and even linebacker Don Davis saw time at safety.

In the end, the Patriots played their game in their conditions. The field was a mess, just the way the Patriots like it after Thanksgiving.

"It was a lot of fun playing out there," Bruschi said. "The sloppier the better. Getting your uniform wet and dirty and playing in the mud, that's what you love if you're a football player."

It was not what the Ravens, who play on synthetic grass, loved. Not with Lewis missing. Not with Orlando Brown, their large right tackle, missing with an injury.

Yet it was tied at the half because the Patriots botched the final 1:08.

The Patriots were content to run out the clock. But after Tom Brady took a knee on first down, the Ravens called time. Dillon ran a sweep, but went out of bounds to stop the clock with 56 seconds remaining. On fourth down, Josh Miller punted, and on the play Matt Chatham drew a 15-yard facemask call. Tack on a Bruschi unsportsmanlike conduct penalty, and the Ravens had first and 10 on the Patriot 16.

The Ravens moved it to the 4 with five seconds left, but Boller overthrew Randy Hymes in the end zone, forcing Matt Stover to kick the tying 22-yard field goal.

"I mean, yeah, I probably should have been looking at the clock and staying in-bounds, but, hey, what was the score, 24-3? I don't think it really matters at this point," Dillon said.

The coaches were fuming about the faulty game management.

"I didn't do a really good job with that," coach Bill Belichick said. "We run out of bounds. We got two 15-yard penalties on a punt. All the things you could do wrong, we did wrong."

"I think guys just knew they had to play better," Harrison said. "We were talking about it, but we remained pretty calm and knew if we went out there and played our game we'd be all right in the second half."

That's what they did.

Vinatieri hit a 40-yard field goal with 11:22 to play in the third after the Patriots took the second-half kickoff and made three first downs, two on Dillon runs. The Ravens had two three-and-outs in the quarter, unable to mount anything against the Patriot front seven.

The Pats had a touchdown (Brady to David Patten for 23 yards) called back with 7:46 remaining on offensive interference on Patten, and settled for the 48-yarder by Vinatieri at the lighthouse end of the field, where the wind wasn't quite as strong.

"If it was the other end of the field, we probably wouldn't have attempted it," Vinatieri said. "We had set the parameters before the game during the warmups. On that kick, I really didn't even make an adjustment for the wind." ⌐

BY NICK CAFARDO

In a laugher

42-15

NE	14	7	21	0
CLE	0	7	0	8

12/5/2004
64°, PARTLY SUNNY
PAUL BROWN STADIUM
CLEVELAND

THEIR MEMBERSHIP IN THE NFL ELITE entitles the Patriots to a gimme from time to time, like the 42-15 shellacking of the hapless Cleveland Browns.

The Patriots piled up 225 yards rushing (100 from Corey Dillon), 201 yards receiving (74 from David Patten), got a special teams touchdown before the game was 15 seconds old, and were facing a rookie quarterback on a team whose coach and executive vice president re-

signed during the week.

The Patriots are now 11-1, continuing the best start in franchise history, and have won 26 of their last 27 games.

The speedy Bethel Johnson took heed of coach Bill Belichick's message during the week when the coach impressed on the young returner the need to grab momentum early. Evidently, Johnson was all ears, and then he was all legs.

Johnson found an opening near the 20-yard line on the opening kickoff, made a nice cut to the right, and busted loose 93 yards all the way to paydirt, shutting up the Dawg Pound.

"I don't know about quieting them, but the thing I was trying to do was worry about the emotion on our side," Johnson said. "We were coming into a hostile environment in an AFC game. I'd been close to breaking one a few times, and I know it's frustrating not to be able to do it, but we got good blocking up front, I found a seam and ran it."

The Browns are so porous that by the time Adam Vinatieri nailed the 42d point following a 44-yard Tom Brady-to-Patten touchdown, it marked the 100th point the Browns had given up in two weeks.

"All I know is that I'm having a lot of fun right now," said Troy Brown, who shadowed slot receiver Dennis Northcutt and came up with his second interception of the season — and career — in the fourth quarter. "I think the thing we al-

NEW ENGLAND	FIRST DOWNS	CLEVELAND	RUSHING YARDS	PASSING YARDS	TURNOVERS
	27/15		225/46	187/241	3/4

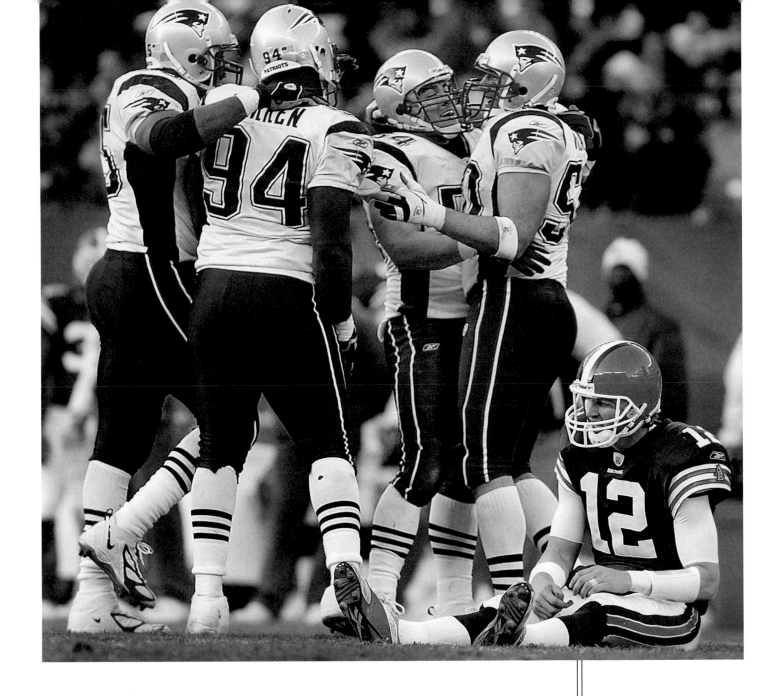

ways keep in mind as a team is that it doesn't matter what the score is, or what the team's record is we're playing, if you let your guard down, you're going to get beat. You have to play all-out all of the time.

"It's all mental toughness," Brown added. "It's hard to keep that up for an entire season and the teams that can do that are the teams who have a chance to win it all at the end."

Dillon earned his total on 18 carries and scored two touchdowns, but he left the game with a leg injury in the second

quarter. Knowing he was 2 yards shy of 100, he campaigned to get back in and got his wish with a 2-yard carry to reach the century mark. The Patriots ran the ball a season-high 50 times, also utilizing Kevin Faulk, who gained 87 yards on 13 carries, and rookie Cedric Cobbs, who ran for 29 yards on 16 carries.

The Patriots controlled the ball for 39:08, while the Browns were held to 46 yards rushing as rookie quarterback Luke McCown was riddled with blitzes in the second half and sacked three times. He

FROM LEFT, ROMAN PHIFER, TY WARREN, AND TEDY BRUSCHI CROWD AROUND MIKE VRABEL AFTER VRABEL'S THIRD-QUARTER SACK OF CLEVELAND QB LUKE MCCOWN (12). COREY DILLON, AT LEFT, REMINDS SOME RAZZING FANS TO CHECK THE SCORE.

SACKS	PENALTIES	TIME OF POSSESSION	RECORD
3/2	7-60/7-84	39:08/20:52	11-1/3-9

14:46
1ST QUARTER

The Patriots were a prohibitive favorite against the Browns, but a 93-yard return for a touchdown by Bethel Johnson, right, on the opening kickoff seemed to decide the matter 14 seconds into the game. Johnson, who was second in the league in kickoff returns in 2003, was tied for eighth in the 2004 regular season.

managed 277 yards with two TD passes and two interceptions in his debut.

Randall Gay picked up a Wiliam Green fumble (forced by Richard Seymour) and raced 41 yards for a score with 13:27 remaining in the third quarter, making it 28-7 after the Browns had pulled within two touchdowns on Antonio Bryant's 16-yard catch late in the first half.

The Patriots scored in every phase of the game.

"That's what we needed," said Brady, who completed 11 of 20 passes for 157 yards, a touchdown, and an interception before giving way to Rohan Davey with 1:56 remaining in the third quarter. "We were looking for a big play to start the game and Bethel provided that for us. Our secondary made big plays. 'Blue' [Gay's nickname] had a great game. It was a total team effort."

The Browns, who are going nowhere this season, are committed to starting Mc-Cown the rest of the way — even though Jeff Garcia has been upgraded to probable with a shoulder sprain.

When the game was still close early, Mc-Cown made some critical mistakes.

Dillon fumbled at his 32, but McCown threw into double coverage and Rodney Harrison made an acrobatic pick at the 5-yard line. The Patriots made McCown pay for that gaffe, churning out a 12-play, 95-yard drive on which Dillon ground up 42 yards and capped it with a 4-yard run with 16 seconds to go in the first quarter, giving New England the 14-0 lead.

After the kickoff the Browns marched to the Patriots' 29, where they faced a fourth and 5. New coach Terry Robiskie decided to go for it, but McCown managed only a 2-yard completion to Northcutt, halting the drive.

The Patriots proceeded to march 72 yards in 10 plays, with the key being a Browns' penalty of 39 yards for pass interference. That gave the Patriots a first-and-goal at the 5-yard line. Dillon capped the drive with a 1-yard plunge.

The Browns followed by putting together an 11-play, 70-yard drive in their 2-minute offense, in which McCown looked his best. His connection with Bryant was fluky in that the ball hit off Frisman Jackson's hands and eluded Brown, who was defending, falling into Bryant's hands.

The second half would be all Pats. ◄

The defense picks its spots

BY NICK CAFARDO

35-28

CIN	0	14	7	7
NE	7	21	7	0

12/12/2004
39°, PARTLY CLOUDY
GILLETTE STADIUM
FOXBOROUGH

WHEN A TEAM IS 12-1, CLINCHING A playoff berth and the AFC East title in spite of allowing almost 500 yards of offense, what else can one do but project this type of performance down the road to more meaningful games?

What if the Patriots' defense allows almost 500 yards to the Indianapolis Colts, or to Pittsburgh, in January? What if they play a team whose quarterback doesn't throw an interception for a touchdown, as Carson Palmer did in a 35-28 Patriots win over Cincinnati at Gillette Stadium?

"The offense definitely bailed out the defense," Patriots defensive lineman Richard Seymour said after the win.

On the day offensive coordinator Charlie Weis accepted the Notre Dame head coaching job, New England's offense put up 28 points and certainly made Weis look good (an offense minus Notre Dame's own David Givens, who sustained a leg injury Saturday).

Yet the defense did three very important things. Asante Samuel intercepted a Palmer pass and ran it back 34 yards for a touchdown. Rodney Harrison hit Rudi Johnson and caused him to fumble on Cincinnati's opening drive at the Patriots' 12. And Troy Brown intercepted a Jon Kitna end-zone pass in the fourth quarter.

"We just can't let a team go up and down the field like that," Harrison said. "We just weren't able to stop them. We're happy to get the win, don't get me wrong. But we can and have to play a lot better than this. That was a very explosive team we faced. It's not anything we didn't anticipate, but we have to do a better job stopping them."

Nor was it a great day for the Patriots' special teams, which allowed a fake field goal for a score by punter Kyle Larson, who took the snap and rambled 11 yards for the Bengals' third score with 3:10 left in the third quarter.

But, as in most games when the Patriots aren't artistically strong, they wait for the other team to shoot itself in the foot. The Bengals had a very good chance to score on their opening possession. Palmer, who left the game late in the third quarter with a knee sprain, engineered an impressive drive before Johnson coughed up the ball on a good smack from Harrison, allowing Willie McGinest to recover.

The tone was set right there.

"You've got to get points there," Palmer said. "Obviously points would have been big. We had two turnovers in the red zone and you just can't do that against the Su-

	FIRST DOWNS	RUSHING YARDS	PASSING YARDS	TURNOVERS
NEW ENGLAND / CINCINNATI	22/26	94/150	257/328	0/3

per Bowl champions. We left points out there, and that makes all the difference in a game like this."

Tom Brady, who came out of a mini slump in his previous two games to complete 18 of 26 passes for 260 yards and two touchdowns (48 yards to David Patten and 17 to Christian Fauria) for a 127.1 quarterback rating, made the Bengals hurt a little bit more.

He directed a 13-play, 84-yard drive, making five first downs, three in a row to begin the drive. They came on pass plays of 23 yards to Deion Branch and 16 yards to Patten, and in between Corey Dillon, facing his old teammates for the first time in the regular season, rumbled for 16 yards. Dillon carried 22 times on the day, gaining 88 yards.

The drive culminated with power football — Dillon getting a lead block from Mike Vrabel to get in from the 1-yard line

with 5:08 remaining in the first quarter.

Instead of being ahead, the Bengals were forced to play from behind, though they appeared unbothered. They tied the score early in the second quarter when Palmer found tight end Matt Schobel in the end zone from 2 yards out.

Then came two scores in 12 seconds for the Patriots. Brady connected with Patten on the 48-yarder when Patten beat his defender and Brady laid it out there perfectly. On the first play after the kickoff, Palmer tried to throw a sideline pass to T.J. Houshmandzadeh, but he didn't put enough mustard on the ball and Samuel made the play and went in untouched.

"I just read the quarterback," said Samuel. "It was a three-step drop. I read it, broke on it, and made the play."

There was the chance for the Patriots' defense to end this game early with its usual smothering ways, particularly

CHRISTIAN FAURIA TAKES TO THE AIR AFTER CATCHING A 17-YARD TD PASS FROM TOM BRADY. IT MADE THE SCORE 35-14, BUT THE PATRIOTS ENDED UP SQUEAKING PAST THE BENGALS.

SACKS	PENALTIES	TIME OF POSSESSION	RECORD
0/1	2-13/9-75	26:49/33:11	12-1/6-7

12:38
4TH QUARTER

The Bengals were trailing, 35-21, early in the fourth quarter, but threatening to get closer, facing a third and goal at the Patriots' 10-yard line. It was just the time for receiver-turned-defensive back Troy Brown to make a stand. Bengals QB Jon Kitna took a short drop, looked right, then threw back to the left toward Chad Johnson. Brown had drifted back, staying in front of Johnson, knowing he had help from safety Eugene Wilson and linebacker Tedy Bruschi. Kitna's pass came underneath Johnson and Brown made the easy interception 2 yards into the end zone.

against the run, but Johnson, who gained 89 yards on 24 carries, kept churning away. The Bengals pulled within one score when Palmer dumped a 5-yard pass over Randall Gay to Chad Johnson to cap a 69-yard drive with 2:31 left in the half.

That's often too much time to leave on the clock when you're playing the Patriots, who seem to enjoy scoring right before the half to give them an edge. Such was the case against Cincinnati.

Bethel Johnson made a 38-yard kick return to the Patriots' 47, and Brady could smell an opportunity.

Two runs by Dillon accounted for 17 yards, and a Patten catch along the sideline for 20 yards set the stage for Kevin Faulk rambling in from the 4 with 22 seconds left on a nice block from guard Stephen Neal.

"I think he could have done it without me," Neal said. "I get excited when I'm pulling and I see a guy I have to block with a number in the 20s."

Brady led the Patriots 75 yards after the second-half kickoff, capping the drive by tossing it out there for Fauria to make the catch in the end zone from 17 yards

JUST 12 SECONDS AFTER DAVID PATTEN'S SECOND-QUARTER TOUCHDOWN CATCH, ASANTE SAMUEL FINDS THE END ZONE ON A 34-YARD INTERCEPTION RETURN AFTER PICKING OFF A CARSON PALMER FLAT PASS.

out. The Patriots were in a double tight end set, and both Fauria and Jed Weaver were open, according to Brady.

"The throw was a little high and [Fauria] went up and got it," said Brady. "It was a good play to start the third quarter."

After the Bengals scored on the fake field goal, the Pats couldn't pull off a trick play on fourth and 1 at the Bengals' 39 with 6:41 remaining. Larry Izzo was lined up as a blocker as punter Josh Miller moved out wide and Izzo went under center, took the direct snap, and was stuffed for no gain.

"I take full responsibility for it," Izzo said. "I should have taken a delay [penalty]. That's my bad."

Kitna pulled the Bengals close with 3:50 to play with a 27-yard touchdown pass to Kelley Washington, who snared the ball over Earthwind Moreland.

All the Bengals needed to do was stop the Patriots when they gave them the ball back with 3:44 left. But eight plays later, Brady was taking a knee for the final time, running out the clock. For all the talk about the Patriots' defense, it was the Bengals who couldn't make a big stop when it counted most.

BY NICK CAFARDO

Squished

29-28

| NE | 7 | 7 | 7 | 7 |
| MIA | 7 | 3 | 7 | 12 |

12/20/2004
52°, CLEAR
PRO PLAYER STADIUM
MIAMI

HELL WAS FREEZING OVER. PIGS WERE flying. And the Dolphins were beating the Patriots.

When A.J. Feeley found 6-foot-2-inch receiver Derrius Thompson for a 21-yard scoring pass over 5-10 Troy Brown with 1:23 remaining in the game on a fourth and 10, it capped an amazing night for the lowly Miami Dolphins, who staged their Super Bowl at Pro Player Stadium in a 29-28 victory, handing the Patriots their second loss of the season.

The winning score was set up by Tom Brady's third of four interceptions, to linebacker Brendon Ayanbadejo after Jason Taylor had Brady in his grasp on third down inside the Patriots 20. Brady was trying to get the ball to Daniel Graham, in what surely would have clinched it for the Patriots.

Brady still had 1:17 to lead a comeback, but he was sacked by David Bowens for a 9-yard loss and then free safety Arturo Freeman finished it off with the fourth INT on a pass intended for David Givens at the Patriot 37.

"They got cocky today," Freeman said. "They felt they were the defending champions and could make plays all over the field. We are the only team, if you check history, that New England has a problem playing against."

For the first time since Halloween, when they bowed to the Steelers, the Patriots experienced the opposing quarterback taking a knee to end the game. And for the first time this year the Patriots were second fiddle to the Steelers, who are 13-1 to the Patriots' 12-2. The Dolphins improved to 3-11.

Brown blamed himself for the Thompson catch, saying, "I didn't make the play. I've got to do everything I can to keep him from catching that."

The New England locker room was understandably quiet after the game. Brady, who was sacked twice and knocked down numerous times, said, "I found out a long time ago you're not going to win too many games throwing four interceptions."

Of the interception to Ayanbadejo, Brady said, "It was just a bad play. I thought I could get it to Dan. I thought I had time to throw, but my arm got ripped and I just pulled it right to the guy. It's just not a good play, and if we want to win games we can't do that. We've got to play better and it starts with me."

Brady's poor night overshadowed a good game by Corey Dillon, who carried 26 times for 121 yards. Dillon had his

| NEW ENGLAND | FIRST DOWNS 24/18 | MIAMI | RUSHING YARDS 166/52 | PASSING YARDS 156/179 | TURNOVERS 4/1 |

TOM BRADY IS HEADED FOR A FALL, AS ARE THE PATS, AFTER THIS ILL-ADVISED PASS WAS PICKED OFF BY MIAMI'S BRENDON AYANBADEJO.

SACKS	PENALTIES	TIME OF POSSESSION	RECORD
4/2	4-53/9-67	35:06/24:54	12-2/3-11

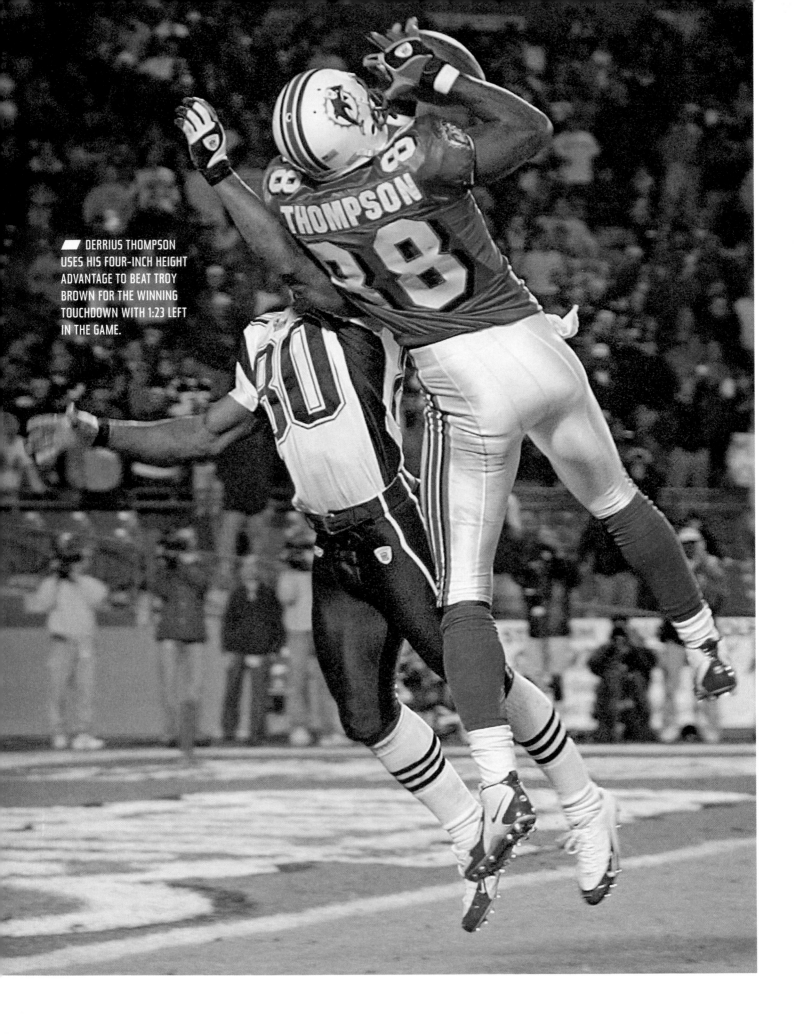

DERRIUS THOMPSON USES HIS FOUR-INCH HEIGHT ADVANTAGE TO BEAT TROY BROWN FOR THE WINNING TOUCHDOWN WITH 1:23 LEFT IN THE GAME.

eighth 100-yard game and helped eat up 4:57 of a 65-yard drive that gave the Patriots a 28-17 lead with 3:59 left to play.

Dillon set up the score with a 20-yard rumble up the middle to the Dolphins' 2, from where Brady threw his third TD pass of the night, this one to Graham.

But the Dolphins were able to respond in 1:52, going 68 yards on seven plays. The drive was capped by Sammy Morris's 1-yard plunge after Patriots safety Rodney Harrison had been flagged for interference in the end zone against Chris Chambers. The Dolphins failed to execute the 2-point conversion, and there was 2:07 left on the clock.

The Patriots were unable to run that out and the Dolphins were not to be denied.

"We had an 11-point lead and we blew it," said Harrison. "They made plays in the end and we made mistakes. We were prepared to play, we just didn't execute. It's not the end of the world. We're obviously disappointed."

Strange events began to unfold in the second half that led one to believe the Dolphins, trailing only 14-10 at the half, continued to mean business. Sammy Knight picked off his second Brady pass at the Dolphins' 10 and returned it 32 yards, which led to the Dolphins taking a 17-14 lead with 6:50 remaining in the third quarter.

The Dolphins got some hard running from Travis Minor, while Feeley (22 for 35 for 198 yards and one touchdown) continued to hit key passes against the ailing Patriots secondary, which also lost Randall Gay (wind knocked out of him). Feeley connected with Chambers on a key 9-yard first-down catch to the Patriots 15. Willie McGinest incurred a facemask penalty while bringing down Feeley on the next play, and before you knew it, Minor was launching himself into the end zone from a yard out, giving the Dolphins the lead.

It marked only the third time all season that the Patriots had trailed in the third quarter.

On the Patriots' next series, the Dolphins' Morlon Greenwood committed a 15-yard facemask penalty at the end of a 10-yard pass from Brady to Graham, and then Sam Madison was called for unnecessary roughness, which put the Patriots at the Dolphins' 2 with a first down. Two plays later, Brady, with an enormous amount of time, spotted Dillon moving along the goal line and hit him with a 2-

yard pass to make it 21-17.

The touchdown was Dillon's second of the night and 12th of the season. His first-quarter scoring run gave him a personal best, and he earned another $500,000 bonus for breaking the 1,350-yard plateau in the first half.

The Patriots had made their customary first-drive march, going 77 yards on nine plays. They used a steady dose of Dillon, starting the game with an 18-yard pop on a pitchout around left end behind tackle Matt Light. Dillon carried 31 yards in all, but the big play was Brady's lob over the middle to a wide-open Kevin Faulk, who had beaten a linebacker and went in untouched from 31 yards out.

One thing Bill Belichick didn't want to do was give the Dolphins any inspiration. But that happened when Miami punt returner Wes Welker caught Josh Miller's 44-yarder late in the first quarter and raced down the left sideline for 71 yards after a juke of Miller set him free.

Welker, who had been a mediocre eighth in the AFC with an 8.9-yards-per-return average, was unable to score because Je'Rod Cherry got a piece of Welker's knee after being blocked near the 10-yard line. Welker stumbled 2 yards shy of paydirt. It took Morris one handoff from Feeley to bust into the end zone with 6:30 remaining in the first quarter, tying the score at 7.

"A return like that is a big momentum swing, especially in the NFL," Welker said. "Any time you can get a big play like that, it puts the team in good position to score and win a game."

Dillon, Faulk, and Patrick Pass carried on 10 of the 12 plays in a 50-yard drive in the second quarter. A 3-yard score by Dillon gave the Patriots a 14-7 lead with 7:01 left in the half.

The Dolphins, who kept showing signs they could solve the Patriots' defense, made it 14-10 when Olindo Mare hit a 30-yard field goal with 1:52 remaining.

It's usually the Patriots who score just before each half. Not so this time.

Brady got the ball back with 1:45 remaining, usually plenty of time, but this time he was intercepted while trying to throw it deep as Knight emerged with the ball. The Dolphins got it back at their 21, but could only get 2 first downs and had to punt. ◄

COLTS
CARDINALS
BILLS
DOLPHINS
SEAHAWKS
JETS
STEELERS
RAMS
BILLS
CHIEFS
RAVENS
BROWNS
BENGALS
DOLPHINS
JETS
49ERS

BY NICK CAFARDO

Intentional grounding

23-7

NE	0	13	3	7
NYJ	0	0	0	7

12/26/2004
30°, OVERCAST
GIANTS STADIUM
EAST RUTHERFORD

THE MESSAGE WILLIE MCGINEST AND the other Patriots received from the coaches was simple — win the game and earn a bye week. It wasn't exactly something they needed to be hit over the head with, but they knew it was there for the taking.

"All week long the coaches told us, 'This is what you've played all season for,' and they were right," said McGinest. "We prepared well all week. We put last week behind us and we went out and did what we're capable of as a team. We put together three phases of the game and we beat a good team, a divisional rival, on their turf."

After completing the 23-7 shellacking of the Jets, coach Bill Belichick decided that talk of bye weeks was the old message, and any discussion of the topic should be eliminated from the players' conversation.

The goal for the last week of the season was a chance to match last year's 14-2 mark by beating the San Francisco 49ers at Gillette Stadium.

"It's significant because we haven't had a week off since early in the season," said

wide receiver/defensive back Troy Brown. "It's always important to achieve these goals along the way. We got one today. We responded to what we needed to do."

And the Jets sure didn't.

The Jets have been hearing questions all season by members of the New York media about their problem beating elite teams. The questioning usually gets a surly reaction from the players.

A couple of weeks back, when asked about beating "soft" teams, New York center Kevin Mawae said, "San Diego is 9-3. We beat them on the road. San Diego is not a good team right now? Are they a good team right now? They are a playoff contender. We beat a playoff contender on the road. We're 9-3. Put that in your [notebook]. Ridiculous."

Then Chad Pennington chastised the media last week because they kept writing that he can't beat a good team. The Patriots' dominance yesterday, meaning the Jets missed a chance to clinch a wildcard berth, didn't make Pennington's and Mawae's cases look very strong.

Along with an effective job by the Patriots' front seven, Tom Brady rebounded marvelously from a four-interception performance against the Dolphins in Miami, taking the 77,975 fans at the Meadowlands out of the game early on a frigid day.

Brady tossed two touchdowns and threw for 264 yards with no interceptions in an impressive road performance.

	FIRST DOWNS		RUSHING YARDS	PASSING YARDS	TURNOVERS
NEW ENGLAND	21/17	NEW YORK	114/46	258/233	0/3

MIND IF I CUT IN? TEDY BRUSCHI PICKS OFF A PASS INTENDED FOR SANTANA MOSS, ONE OF TWO NEW ENGLAND INTERCEPTIONS OFF JETS QB CHAD PENNINGTON.

SACKS	PENALTIES	TIME OF POSSESSION	RECORD
3/1	3-25/4-20	35:48/24:12	13-2/10-5

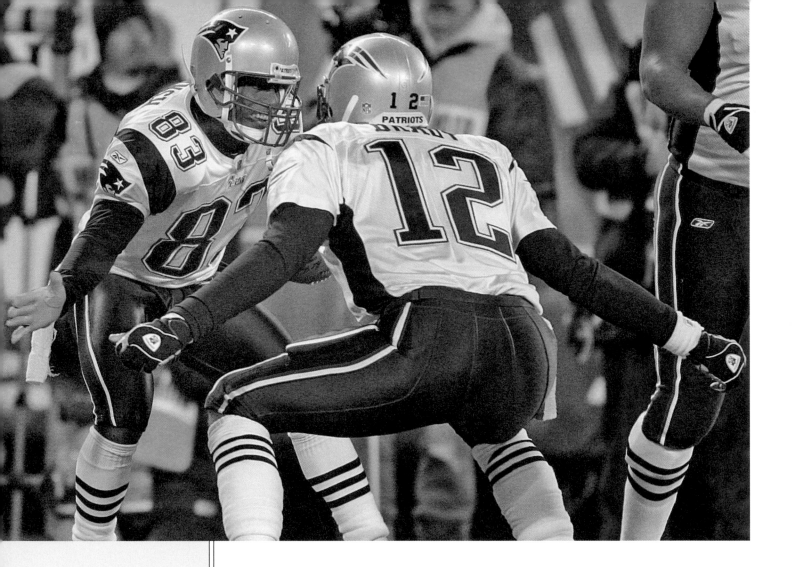

PLAY OF THE
GAME
12:42
4TH QUARTER

Ahead 16-0, the Patriots had a shot to break the game open. On second and goal at the Jets' 6, WR Deion Branch (83) ran straight at Terrell Buckley before cutting inside. Buckley fell, Branch had an easy TD catch, and the Pats had a 23-0 lead.

The only hostility from the fans was directed at their own players (the Jets were booed off the field at halftime) and the play-calling of offensive coordinator Paul Hackett.

Also drawing jeers was Pennington, who threw two interceptions and fumbled, all of which led to Patriots scores. Pennington had 252 yards passing, but 147 came after the score was 23-0.

"[The Patriots] just came down here, and as I told our football team, they flat-out kicked our behinds — on offense, defense, and special teams," said Jets coach Herman Edwards. "That is how it all boils down. We knew what was at stake. We needed to win a game at home to get back into the playoffs and we didn't do it."

The opposite was true of Belichick's 11. The coach had his team well-prepared. There would be no references to offensive coordinator Charlie Weis's head being at Notre Dame, where he recently was named the coach. There was no talk of a Brady slump, or poor play by the secondary, even though Ty Law was a pregame scratch when it appeared he had had a chance to play. The defense held Curtis Martin, the league's leading rusher entering the game, to 33 yards on 13 carries.

With 29 carries for 89 yards, Corey Dillon broke the Patriots' season rushing record, previously held by Martin, and three field goals by Adam Vinatieri gave him a personal high for points in a season. The Patriots controlled every aspect of the game, including time of possession, 35:48 to 24:12.

On a day when they retired Joe Klecko's No. 73, the Jets had one of their darkest moments of the season, while the Patriots rebounded.

It was hard to pinpoint exactly where the teams parted ways yesterday, but the second quarter was a good place to start. Vinatieri kicked a 28-yard field goal with 7:47 remaining in the second through a tough crosswind.

But even before that, Tedy Bruschi seemed to take the life out of the Jets on the first series when it appeared New York was going to march downfield for an opening-drive score. Bruschi intercepted Pennington's weak throw, intended for Santana Moss at the Patriot 26, and returned it 36 yards to the Jets' 38. Even though the Patriots didn't take advantage, the damage it had done was clear. It became a game of field position, and then the Patriots took it away.

"They drove the ball on us a little bit and we were able to switch the field position with the interception," Bruschi said. "Willie made a key third-down stop for us, and we made them punt. Our offense took a little time to get going, but they did."

The absence of injured John Abraham took away some of the Jets' ability to chase Brady and allowed the quarterback to get comfortable in his surroundings. The Patriots' drive to the field goal took 7:18, with a good dose of Dillon and a 10-yard run by Patrick Pass mixed in. With 6:02 remaining in the second, the Patriots began their first touchdown drive. A huge play was Brady finding David Givens for a 35-yard catch to the Jets' 17. Givens had been out of the offensive mix for a few weeks, but was very much part of things in this game.

Two plays later, Brady found a wide-open Daniel Graham in the middle of the end zone for a 10-0 Patriots lead.

The Patriots got three more points on Vinatieri's 29-yard field goal with 7 seconds remaining in the half, getting the ball back with 1:13 remaining and moving 32 yards. Brady connected with Deion Branch on a 21-yard pass to put New England in good position at the Jets' 11 after Brown had made a 23-yard punt return to the Jets' 43.

"That was huge, because we got good field position and were able to make it a two-touchdown game pretty much," Brown said.

When the Patriots recovered a fumble on the ensuing kickoff, which had been hit into the ground by Vinatieri, the kicker attempted a 50-yarder. But although it had the distance, the wind carried it wide left.

Another Vinatieri field goal after a 79-yard drive in the third quarter, which ate up more than seven minutes, added to the Jets' misery. The final calamity for the Jets came when Pennington was intercepted by Eugene Wilson at the Jets' 39 seconds into the fourth quarter. Wilson returned it to the 15, and four plays later the Patriots put even more distance between them and the Jets with a 6-yard scoring toss from Brady to Branch.

"We don't focus on wins too much and we don't focus on losses too much," Bruschi said. "We try to put it behind us as quickly as we can and move on. Maybe it was good that it was a Monday night game and we didn't have time to dwell on it."

Nor could they dwell on the bye they had just earned. 🏈

EUGENE WILSON SAVORS HIS FOURTH-QUARTER INTERCEPTION, WHICH HE RETURNED 24 YARDS TO THE JETS' 15-YARD LINE, SETTING UP A TOUCHDOWN CATCH BY DEION BRANCH, LEFT.

Fitting finish

BY NICK CAFARDO

21-7

SF	7	0	0	0
NE	0	7	7	7

1/2/2005
32°, PARTLY CLOUDY
GILLETTE STADIUM
FOXBOROUGH

THE COACH PERHAPS HAS GOTTEN the biggest piece of the credit pie for the Patriots' success the last four seasons, but yesterday Bill Belichick gladly cut the largest piece for his players for enduring a season of injuries and the pressures associated with staying atop the mountain during a second consecutive 14-win season.

"For what they've been through this year, I think you have to give a lot of credit to the players for their diligence, their perseverance, and for battling all the way through," Belichick said following a 21-7 victory over the 49ers in the season finale at Gillette Stadium. "It has been a long season and they played well enough today and we're happy with that. It's on to the playoffs."

"I don't know who we play next," Belichick said. "It doesn't make any difference. Whoever it is will be pretty good and we know that. I'm glad we ended up on top and ended up with a 14-2 record. I thought the players deserved that for what they have done this year."

There was a sense all week the players wanted to end on a high note, match last season's 14-win total, and go undefeated at home in back-to-back seasons.

A captains' meeting with Belichick late in the week bore that out; the captains spoke of needing some momentum heading into the playoffs.

Besides the win, the other major highlights were escaping the game with all of their major players healthy, and Corey Dillon eclipsing the 1,600-yard mark to earn a $375,000 incentive.

"This is good for us," said left tackle Matt Light. "We haven't been able to take the foot off the pedal all season. This week will be a well-deserved break for us."

Most of the starters came out at some point late in the game, although they probably had to play longer than expected because it took them a while to get going. The Patriots trailed, 7-0, for the first time in the last 24 games.

It wasn't until the start of the fourth quarter, with New England driving for its third score, that Rohan Davey relieved Tom Brady. Brady threw 30 passes, completing 22 for 226 yards and two touchdowns.

Dillon left after eclipsing the 1,600-yard mark when he went off right guard for 29 yards to the 14 with 10:19 left in the third quarter. With 116 yards, he went over the 100-yard mark for the ninth time this season, and helped the Patriots run for a 4.07-yards-per-carry average, the best since the 1985 team.

The Patriots ran it 524 times for 2,134

	FIRST DOWNS		RUSHING YARDS	PASSING YARDS	TURNOVERS
NEW ENGLAND / SAN FRANCISCO	23/15		174/135	231/183	3/2

ON TOP FOR GOOD: DEION BRANCH AND TOM BRADY MAKE CONNECTIONS AFTER COMBINING FOR AN 8 YARD TOUCHDOWN AND A 14-7 LEAD. PATRICK PASS (35) GETS IN ON THE ACT.

SACKS	PENALTIES	TIME OF POSSESSION	RECORD
1/1	4-37/7-64	29:12/30:48	14-2/2-14

The Patriots took the lead for good when Tom Brady hit Deion Branch on a quick 8-yard strike midway through the third quarter. The key to the four-play, 51-yard drive was a 29-yard run by Corey Dillon that put the Pats deep in 49er territory.

yards this season, throwing it 485 times for 3,750 gross yards.

Dillon returned at the start of the fourth quarter, coinciding with the appearance of Davey, and scored his 12th rushing touchdown.

"[Running backs coach] Ivan [Fears] told me to go back in," Dillon said. "I don't know what the big deal is. I don't find it weird at all."

Dillon escaped his 14-carry workload with no injuries. He seemed relatively happy after the game, as did all the Patriots, who finally can exhale for a week.

Most of the players talked about having such a successful season despite missing top players from the lineup. Defensive end Richard Seymour and cornerback Ty Law were held out, and the hope was that both would be ready for the playoffs in two weeks, although their status is uncertain.

The Patriots amassed 174 yards rushing on 28 carries. New faces such as Cedric Cobbs and Rabih Abdullah carried the ball late in the game. Jarvis Green started at Seymour's right defensive end spot. Don Davis started at free safety, with Eugene Wilson getting the day off. Randall Gay, who had missed last week's game because of an arm injury, got some playing time.

Bethel Johnson returned a punt for a touchdown, but it was called back because of a penalty. Je'Rod Cherry, who was cut two weeks ago and then re-signed, downed two punts inside the 5. Former starter Russ Hochstein saw some time on the offensive line. Tully Banta-Cain played outside linebacker and recovered a fumble.

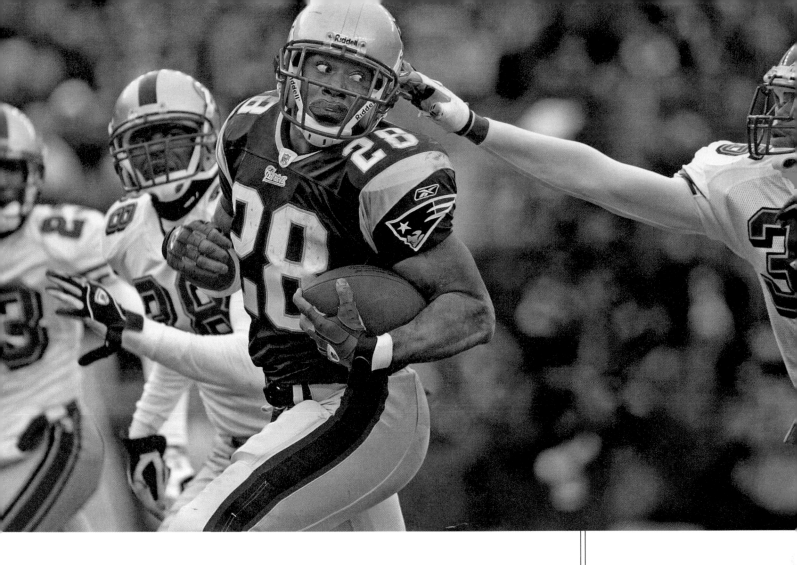

The 49ers did have the early momentum, taking advantage of an interception by free safety Dwaine Carpenter at the San Francisco 47, which he returned 31 yards to the Patriots' 22. It took quarterback Ken Dorsey five plays to get the worst team in football into the end zone, on a 4-yard catch by Steve Bush with 2:48 remaining in the first quarter.

The 49ers had a chance to go ahead, 10-0, and really take over, but Todd Peterson hit the right upright from 39 yards out on a field goal try in the second quarter.

"Any time you play a team like that, you have no room for mistakes," 49ers receiver Curtis Conway said. "I think what hurt them early was that they had two turnovers. Then they realized we had come to play, so they turned it up a notch to get what they had to do to win."

The Patriots took over on their 29 after the missed kick, and Brady and Dillon found their rhythms. Dillon carried three times for 36 yards, and Brady hit Christian Fauria for 11 and David Givens for 22.

A false start by Mike Vrabel pushed the Patriots back to the 7, but Dillon got 6 yards back before Brady found Vrabel alone on the left side for 6 points. Adam Vinatieri's conversion made it 7-7.

It was all Patriots in the second half. Dillon's 29-yard burst started things. Brady completed a 6-yard pass to Fauria and then finished the drive with an 8-yarder to Deion Branch, making it 14-7.

The 49ers came back, but Maurice Hicks fumbled at the Patriot 34 late in the third quarter, and the Patriots turned that into their third and final score. Brady started the drive, then Davey took over. He handed off twice to Dillon, who took care of the final 14 yards of the drive, scoring from the 6.

While it was termed a meaningless game during the week, Brady said, "You can say it doesn't mean everything, but it does mean something. It means something to us. We are 14-2, one of the three teams in history to have back-to-back 14-2 seasons."

◼ COREY DILLON PULLS AWAY FROM SAN FRANCISCO'S DWAINE CARPENTER FOR A 29-YARD SCAMPER. THE RUN PUT DILLON OVER 100 YARDS FOR THE GAME, THE NINTH TIME HE REACHED THE CENTURY MARK IN RUSHING YARDS IN 2004.

◼ MIKE VRABEL CLUTCHES THE BALL AFTER A 1-YARD TD CATCH THAT EVENED THE SCORE AT 7 IN THE SECOND QUARTER.

2004 ROSTER

#	NAME	POS	HT	WT	AGE	YR	WHEN/HOW ACQUIRED	COLLEGE
4	Adam Vinatieri	K	6-0	202	32	9	1996 Rookie free agent	South Dakota State
6	Rohan Davey	QB	6-2	245	26	3	2002 Draft – Rd. 4	Louisiana State
8	Josh Miller	P	6-4	225	34	9	2004 Free agent (Pit)	Arizona
10	Kevin Kasper	WR	6-1	202	27	4	2004 Free agent (Arz)	Iowa
12	Tom Brady	QB	6-4	225	27	5	1999 Draft – Rd. 6	Michigan
13	Jim Miller	QB	6-2	225	33	10	2004 Free agent (TB)	Michigan State
21	Randall Gay	CB	5-11	186	22	R	2004 Rookie free agent	Louisiana State
22	Asante Samuel	CB	5-10	185	23	2	2003 Draft – Rd. 4	Central Florida
24	Ty Law	CB	5-11	200	30	10	1995 Draft – Rd. 1	Michigan
26	Eugene Wilson	DB	5-10	195	24	2	2003 Draft – Rd. 2	Illinois
27	Rabih Abdullah	RB	6-0	235	29	7	2004 Free agent (Chi)	Lehigh
28	Corey Dillon	RB	6-1	225	30	8	2003 Trade (Cin)	Washington
29	Earthwind Moreland	CB	5-10	182	27	3	2004 Free agent (Cle)	Georgia Southern
30	Je'Rod Cherry	DB	6-1	210	31	9	2001 Free agent (Phi)	California
31	Hank Poteat	CB	5-10	192	27	4	2004 Free agent (Car)	Pittsburgh
33	Kevin Faulk	RB	5-8	202	28	6	1999 Draft – Rd. 2	Louisiana State
34	Cedric Cobbs	RB	6-0	225	23	R	2004 Draft – Rd. 4	Arkansas
35	Patrick Pass	FB	5-10	217	27	5	2000 Draft – Rd. 7	Georgia
37	Rodney Harrison	S	6-1	220	32	11	2003 Free agent (SD)	Western Illinois
42	Dexter Reid	S	5-11	203	23	R	2004 Draft – Rd. 4	North Carolina
48	Tully Banta-Cain	LB	6-2	250	24	2	2003 Draft – Rd. 7	California
49	Eric Alexander	LB	6-2	240	22	R	2004 Rookie free agent	Louisiana State
50	Mike Vrabel	LB	6-4	261	29	8	2001 Free agent (Pit)	Ohio State
51	Don Davis	LB	6-1	235	32	9	2003 Free agent (StL)	Kansas
52	Ted Johnson	LB	6-4	253	32	10	1995 Draft – Rd. 2	Colorado
53	Larry Izzo	LB	5-10	228	30	9	2001 Free agent (Mia)	Rice
54	Tedy Bruschi	LB	6-1	247	31	9	1996 Draft – Rd. 3	Arizona
55	Willie McGinest	LB	6-5	270	33	11	1994 Draft – Rd. 1	Southern California
58	Matt Chatham	LB	6-4	250	27	5	2000 Rookie free agent	South Dakota
59	Rosevelt Colvin	LB	6-3	250	27	6	2003 Free agent (Chi)	Purdue
61	Stephen Neal	G	6-4	305	28	3	2001 Rookie free agent	Cal State-Bakersfield
63	Joe Andruzzi	G	6-3	312	29	8	2000 Free agent (GB)	S. Connecticut St.
64	Gene Mruczkowski	G/C	6-2	305	23	2	2003 Rookie free agent	Purdue
66	Lonie Paxton	LS	6-2	260	26	5	2003 Free agent (StL)	Sacramento State
67	Dan Koppen	C	6-2	296	25	2	2003 Draft – Rd. 5	Boston College
71	Russ Hochstein	G	6-4	305	27	4	2002 Rookie free agent	Nebraska
72	Matt Light	T	6-4	305	26	4	2001 Draft – Rd. 2	Purdue
75	Vince Wilfork	DL	6-2	325	24	R	2004 Draft – Rd. 1	Miami (Fla.)
76	Brandon Gorin	T	6-6	308	26	3	2003 Waivers	Purdue

FOR HIS HIGH SCHOOL FOOTBALL TEAM, ASANTE WAS QUARTER-BACK, DEFENSIVE BACK, KICKER, AND PUNTER.

WHILE PLAYING FOR THE CHARGERS, RODNEY DONATED 20 TICKETS FOR EACH HOME GAME TO BIG BROTHERS/BIG SISTERS OF SAN DIEGO

WILLIE REPRESENTS THE R&B GROUP METRO, WHO RECENTLY SIGNED A DEAL WITH INTERSCOPE/A&M RECORDS AND WILL RELEASE AN ALBUM LATER THIS YEAR.

#	NAME	POS	HT	WT	AGE	YR	WHEN/HOW ACQUIRED	COLLEGE
80	Troy Brown	WR	5-10	196	33	12	1993 Draft – Rd. 8	Marshall
81	Bethel Johnson	WR	5-11	200	24	2	2003 Draft – Rd. 2	Texas A&M
82	Daniel Graham	TE	6-3	257	25	3	2002 Draft – Rd. 1	Colorado
83	Deion Branch	WR	5-9	193	25	3	2002 Draft – Rd. 2	Louisville
85	Jed Weaver	TE	6-4	258	28	6	2004 Free agent (Den)	Oregon
86	David Patten	WR	5-10	190	30	8	2001 Free agent (Cle)	Western Carolina
87	David Givens	WR	6-0	215	24	3	2002 Draft – Rd. 7	Notre Dame
88	Christian Fauria	TE	6-4	250	33	10	2001 Free agent (Sea)	Colorado
91	Marquise Hill	DE	6-6	300	22	R	2004 Draft – Rd. 2	Louisiana State
93	Richard Seymour	DL	6-6	310	25	4	2001 Draft – Rd. 1	Georgia
94	Ty Warren	DL	6-5	300	22	2	2003 Draft – Rd. 1	Texas A&M
95	Roman Phifer	LB	6-2	248	36	14	2001 Free agent (NYJ)	UCLA
97	Jarvis Green	DL	6-3	290	25	3	2004 Draft – Rd. 4	Louisiana State
98	Keith Traylor	DT	6-2	340	35	13	2004 Free agent (Chi)	Central State (Okla.)
99	Ethan Kelley	DT	6-2	310	24	1	2003 Draft – Rd. 7	Baylor

PRACTICE SQUAD

#	NAME	POS	HT	WT	AGE	YR	WHEN/HOW ACQUIRED	COLLEGE
18	Cedric James	WR	6-1	197	25	1	2004 Free agent	Texas Christian
19	Ricky Bryant	WR	6-0	185	23	R	2004 Free agent	Hofstra
23	Omare Lowe	DB	6-1	195	26	1	2004 Free agent	Washington
32	Kory Chapman	RB	6-1	202	24	R	2004 Free agent	Jacksonville State
47	Justin Kurpeikis	LB	6-3	254	27	3	2004 Free agent	Penn State
65	Lance Nimmo	T	6-5	303	25	1	2004 Free agent	West Virginia
69	Buck Rasmussen	DL	6-4	285	25	1	2004 Free agent	Nebraska-Omaha
74	Billy Yates	G	6-2	305	24	1	2004 Free agent	Texas A&M

TROY AND FORMER MARSHALL TEAMMATE MIKE BARTRUM OF THE PHILADELPHIA EAGLES SPONSOR A YOUTH FOOTBALL CAMP AND GOLF TOURNAMENT IN THEIR COLLEGE TOWN OF HUNTINGTON, W.VA.

ROMAN IS NAMED AFTER EX-RAMS QB ROMAN GABRIEL AND HIS FATHER CHOSE HIS MIDDLE NAME, ZUBINSKI, OUT OF THE PHONE BOOK. ROMAN NAMED HIS SON, JORDAN, AFTER MICHAEL JORDAN.

HEAD COACH: Bill Belichick

"IT IS CERTAINLY NOT ANY KIND OF SCIENTIFIC THING. IT COMES FROM A COMBINATION OF THE SCOUTS, THE COACHES ... PLUS RECOMMENDATIONS FROM THE SYSTEM THE PLAYERS HAVE BEEN IN AND WHAT THEY HAVE DONE. IT'S ALL ASPECTS OF THE PLAYERS' PERFORMANCE. IT'S HIS WORK ETHIC, HIS COMMITMENT TO FOOTBALL. ALL THAT IS PUT INTO THE POT AND YOU MAKE A DECISION AND PUT A GRADE OR EVALUATION ON THE PLAYER."

ASSISTANTS: Romeo Crennel DEFENSIVE COORDINATOR / Brian Daboll WIDE RECEIVERS / Ivan Fears RUNNING BACKS / Jeff Davidson ASSISTANT OFFENSIVE LINE & TIGHT ENDS / Pepper Johnson DEFENSIVE LINE / Eric Mangini DEFENSIVE BACKS / Josh McDaniels QUARTERBACKS / Matt Patricia COACHING ASSISTANT / Markus Paul ASSISTANT STRENGTH & CONDITIONING / Dean Pees LINEBACKERS / Dante Scarnecchia ASSISTANT HEAD COACH & OFFENSIVE LINE / Brad Seely SPECIAL TEAMS / Cory Undlin COACHING ASSISTANT / Charlie Weis OFFENSIVE COORDINATOR / Mike Woicik STRENGTH & CONDITIONING

2002 ST. LOUIS RAMS

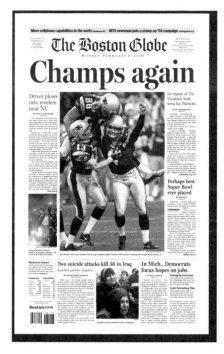

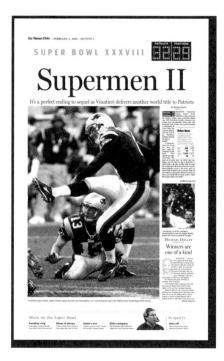

TOM BRADY, WHO EARNED HIS SECOND MVP TROPHY BY REPEATING HIS LATE-GAME HEROICS OF 2002, LEADS THE CHARGE ONTO THE FIELD AT HOUSTON'S RELIANT STADIUM AFTER THE FINAL PLAY OF A WILD 32-29 VICTORY OVER CAROLINA.

2004 CAROLINA PANTHERS

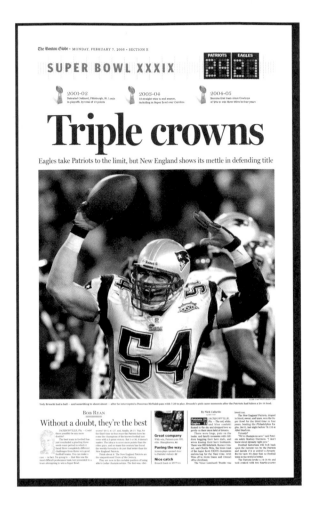